SPACE FOR GOLF

Thomas Neamtu

THE UNINTENDED MANUAL FOR SHENANIGANS AND CUTTING GRASS

Thomas Neamtu

Space for Golf

THE UNINTENDED MANUAL FOR SHENANIGANS

AND CUTTING GRASS

Thomas Neamtu

Thomas Neamtu

First Printing, 2024 – 1,2

ISBN: 979-8338679807

Second Printing

Dedicated to my mother.

Thank you for the support, inspiration & encouragement,

and always having space for golf

Contents

Thomas Neamtu

Introduction

The rules of golf are quite simple. Hit the ball into the hole in the fewest number of shots. The challenge is that the hole is small and hundreds of yards away. Having a variety of clubs at your disposal is the key to victory. First are the woods or drivers. They are used to take the first shot off the tee box, trying to get the maximum distance possible. Next are the Irons, they are used to take the subsequent shots, bringing the ball even closer to the green. Their angled face launches the ball high into the air, providing less distance than the drivers, but moving the ball closer to the hole. Wedges are used to make the final approach or get out of the sand traps that often edge the perimeter of the greens. A skilled wedge shot can often find a good position next to the hole. The putter is finally used for the final taps required to drop the ball into the hole.

It may sound easy enough, but golf is harder than it looks. Although the game is played with others, the true opponent is yourself. A great deal of concentration is required if you are going to make great shots and take less strokes than the game before. Golf is a game of quiet focus and repetition. Just because you can hit the ball a mile does not mean you will find success. The short game, on the greens, is the ultimate equalizer. If you can't sink the putts, your score will increase and the lowest score wins.

Our little course only had a handful of holes that a long drive would suit. Most of the holes were short and required actual control and precision to defeat. If an overzealous player overshot the green, their ball would end up out of bounds, and in someone's yard. If the player hits their shot so hard, the ball might ricochet off the houses, and possibly break a window.

Reading the following stories will not help your game.

I'm hoping you break more windows.

Enjoy.

Chapter 1: Summer of '97

It was time to get a job. I had just finished the 11th grade and wanted to find a summer job. The local golf course seemed like a logical choice. It was close to home and working outside seemed like the best way to spend the summer. My friends went down to the course on Friday after school and got jobs in the pro shop and driving range. I missed out on that opportunity. Fridays I would always go out for dinner with my family. Dad would travel all week, and Fridays were our family night out. We would go to the same restaurant every week and then for groceries. On Saturday I went down to the course with intentions to get a job. I walked into the pro-shop. The room was big. It was filled with the stereotypical brightly colored golf clothes at the front. Towards the back of the room there were rows of the newest golf clubs for sale. To the left of the entrance was a small room used to repair damaged clubs and shoes. The repair room had a door that was cut in half. The bottom half of the door was closed, the top was open, with a man leaning on the closed door. I was greeted as I entered. I was filled with a nervous energy as I walked up to the front counter to inquire about summer employment. I was told that all the front-end pro shop jobs were filled. Before I even had a chance to be disappointed, I was told that I could go down to the maintenance shed to see if they needed anyone. I was pointed in the right direction and exited out of the building.

I walked into the courtyard where all the rentable golf carts were staged. Four carts were freshly cleaned and waiting for players to take them away. The courtyard had two paths; I was instructed to take the one that went past the practice green. The other path would take you towards the street and the first tee box. I walked over a small foot bridge that spanned over a creek. As the pond overflowed, the water would run down a small rock waterfall and into the creek below. I walked past the currently unoccupied practice green. The green was large and had nine holes scattered over its surface. With small flags that stood up straight marking the position of the holes. I started along a well-worn path, made of two parallel tire tracks that had been carved into the ground by countless trips from the golf carts towards the maintenance shed. The left side of the trail was the fairway of the first hole, its lush green grass was ready to be played on. The right side of the trail was unkempt and was home to piles of stone, dirt, and sand. It was the space that divided the first and eighteenth fairways. I walked down the trail for some time before I could see the maintenance shack appear. The taper of the roof just barely visible through a row of trees that grew tall between the fairways. The path began to slope down as I entered the paved lot. The creek ran along the perimeter of the lot and provided a boundary between the course and the maintenance shop area. I could hear the flow of the water as I made my way around to the side of the building to the side with the entrance.

The front door of the building faced into the course; it was lined up with the green from the second hole. The trees were tall and provided a shaded darkness to this side of the building. I opened the metal door, turning the knob and pulling it out towards me. The smell of mechanical grease and grass clipping immediately entered my nose. I could hear voices, so I proceeded into the shop. To the right was a small office with a window. Walking past the window I could see a man sitting at the desk, he was talking to himself. Inside the office was the greens keeper Lee. I stood in the doorway for a moment until my presence caught his attention.

"Hello, I was hoping to get a summer job." I asked with a nervous tremble in my voice. "I was sent here from the pro-shop."

He looked at me, waited a few moments before saying "you start Monday at 6:30 am." and sent me on my way. Well, that was easy. I was excited to get home to tell my parents of my employment success. I left the building and walked back towards the pro-shop.

Mom and Dad were in the kitchen when I got home. I walked into the room; head held high. "I got the job!" I said with excitement.

"Well, that's good." Dad said. "Doing what?" he asked.

"I got a job at the maintenance shop," I told him. "I guess cutting the grass and stuff like that."

Dad hearing the uncertainty in my voice continued with the questions. "How much are you going to get paid?" he asked.

"I don't even know," I said with the revelation that I didn't actually know. "I was just told that I start Monday at 6:30 am." "no questions were asked; no answers were given."

Dad just smiled. "Well, good luck with that." He said, taking a sip from his freshly brewed coffee. "I'm sure Lee will keep you busy all summer."

The alarm clock buzzer went off at 5:45 Monday morning, and I enthusiastically got out of bed and got ready to go to work. I had a quick breakfast. Opened the garage door, got on my bike and went to work. We lived on a hill so the ride to work was quick and easy. The sun was not even up yet, the air was cool but refreshing. I rode to the pro-shop and used the same path I walked days before. I got to the maintenance building, parked my bike near the front door, and went inside.

I was greeted by Lee; he was more friendly at the crack of dawn. "You made it." He said with a welcoming smile. "I have some paperwork for you to fill out." We sat in his office. He rummaged through his desk and pulled out a page for me to add some details too.

"How much will I be getting paid?" I asked looking up from the basic form.

"We start at six dollars and hour," lee said. "There is a dollar an hour increase, each season, if you stay." "But let's not get to far ahead of ourselves just yet." "let's see if you can survive a week." he finished with a mischievous glint in his eyes. I was excited for the six bucks an hour, that was just over minimum wage.

"What will my schedule be like?" I asked.

"We work every day, from 6:30 until 2:30 and on the weekend 6:30 until 10:30." He paused "you get every other weekend off." "The weekends are for the golfers, so we just do the job and get out of the way." He explained.

I nodded in approval, handing over the completed sheet. Lee took the page, looked at it for a moment then quickly put it into his desk. "Head into the lunchroom and meet the rest of the boys," he said gesturing to the door.

I stood up and exited the room. The door to the office looked out into the shop, it was a large space that was divided into a couple of sections. The lights were off in the back, so I could not see what was in the farthest section. The front portion of the room was filled with the parked maintenance golf carts. Each one was equipped with a steel box on the back, used to carry tools or whatever else needed to be moved. There was a work bench that ran along the right wall and curved into the front wall. Making a large, "L" shape. The bench was deep and had lots of space to use when working on projects. There were a few tools on top of the steel topped bench waiting to be repaired. Under the work bench were a bunch of cupboard doors that had been knocked and dinged from years of abuse. There was a big window centered over the workbench. The window was covered with a thick layer of grime, making it almost impossible to see through. To the left of the office was the lunchroom. I could hear the early morning chatter; I took four steps from Lee's office and entered the kitchen. It was a small room, there were chairs lined up long the walls, and a row of home-made lockers along the back. A small round table and a microwave were pushed into the corner. I held my position in the doorway as the other four boys filled up the room. They were all a few years older than me. The group of boys didn't linger long for introductions, they all knew the roles and were off to start the day. I moved out of the doorway as they rushed out to start up the mowers. I asked one of the stragglers which of the machines I was going to pilot. This was met with a smirk and a laugh.

"You probably won't ride a mover all year," they explained, "you have to earn that privilege."

Lee popped his head out of his office door. "Hey Ryan, take Thomas with you today and show him what you do." Before Ryan could make any objection, Lee was back at his desk. I was then teamed up with Ryan. He was going to show me the ropes.

"I, guess its you and me today," Ryan said extending his hand for a proper greeting. Ryan and I got into one of the golf carts that was customized with a work box on the back. The cart was already stocked with garbage bags and some empty boxes. We waited for the others to back out their equipment to clear the path for our cart to exit. Once they were all out of the shop, off we went. The cool morning air biting at my cheeks and ears. We drove down the path towards the pro-shop until we got to the first tee box. Ryan explained that we would be collecting the garbage from all the tee boxes. Weekends were busy at the course and Mondays were one of the largest collection days. I got off the cart and opened one of the garbage bags that were in the front compartment of the cart. The bag was folded neatly. As I walked over to the garbage can I found the edge of the bag, pulling it open and flapping it into the air, the bag expanded to its full potential. I picked up the steel garbage can and dumped it into the bag. The garbage cans were below the ball wash stations. There was a metal spike on the bottom of the expanded metal garbage can, it fits into a small hole, holding the can in place under each of the ball wash stations. I looked down to find the hole and replaced the can into its position. I was then told if I encountered any beer cans that they were to be sorted out of the garbage, and into the provided boxes. The first hole rarely had any beer cans as most players don't start drinking until later into their game. We then proceeded to drive around to the other seventeen tee boxes to collect the rest of Sundays garbage. As we progressed around the course Ryan was telling me stories of how he had worked here a couple of summers ago. But he left for last season to go work at one of the city courses. He ultimately decided to come back and work for Lee. This was closer to home, as his parents' house backed onto the course. He could jump the fence and be at the shop in minutes. As it turns out, the grass is not always greener somewhere else. Although the city course was paying better there was no fun to be had. He went on to say that the greens keeper at the city course would routinely have a mental breakdown and fly into an unhinged rage. If a single blade of grass was missed from being trimmed there would be hell to pay. You would never know if his wrath would fall upon your head for something small and mundane. It was a hard way to spend the summer, looking over your shoulder, waiting to be shouted at. So, Ryan was happy to be back here, where Lee didn't take the job extremely seriously. We were only cutting grass after all. After finishing the collection of all 18 trash cans we returned to the shop for a snack. After the break I was taught how to refill the water coolers.

There was only one tap near the shop that got its water from the city supply. It was located next to the wash station, where the equipment would be cleaned off at the end of every day. Using a clear food grade hose, the two hundred litre water tank would be filled. The tank was mounted on a two-wheel trailer that would be hitched to the back of the golf cart. It was secured to the hitch with a half inch bolt used as hitch pin. The tank would take around fifteen minutes to fill with water. Ryan told me that this was one of the best weekend tasks as it was easy, and only took about an hour to complete. After the tank was filled, we headed out to the first cooler station. It was located at the top of the hill, next to the fifth tee box. The cooler station was just an elevated box, with two doors that housed two coolers. The doors blocked most of each cooler, only the waterspouts were accessible. There was also paper cup dispenser mounted on the outside of the cabinet. We would replace the cone shaped cups as the tank was filling. The doors unlocked using a tiny key. The key was attached to a bright orange foam key chain, the kind used on a boat. So that if you dropped the keys into the water, they would float. The covers were removed with a satisfying suction, and a loud pop as they broke free from the cooler. A pump was attached to the trailer and would get the water into the coolers. Lifting the seat from the golf cart to expose the battery. Electrical jumper cables would be attached, and the pump would start immediately. There was no switch required. It was a simple system. The hose that exited the tank was equipped with an elbow attachment that balanced on the edge of the cooler. If the cooler was completely empty, it would take ten minutes to fill each one. Once the coolers were filled, their lids would be secured, and the cabinet closed and locked. A quick double check to make sure that the keys were not left behind, we proceed to the second water station. It was located at the fourteenth tee box. The process was duplicated at the second location. Once the coolers were both full, we returned to the shop. The trailer was returned to its designated space where it would sit until needed again.

Chapter 2: Kids in Yards

Filling the coolers on the fifth hole always reminded me of a time as a kid, and the trouble we caused. Living on a golf course leads itself to all kinds of free entertainment. One of my friends lived in a house that backed onto the fifth tee box. We would spend countless afternoons bouncing on the trampoline in the center of his yard. Bouncing high watching the golfers. Waiting for the perfect moment right before they made contact with the ball to shout "four!" It was always great fun. Watching their shot as it veered off target caused by the sudden disruption to their concentration. We would laugh hard. Our actions were often met with shaking fists and the threat to tell our parents. These empty treats were no deterrent for our cheap laughter. As the summer wore on the joy of tormenting the golfers started to diminish. We needed to take it up a notch or two, or seven. We started to make our catcalls from the fence. This would take away the barrier that the yard provided. Keeping us close to the action. The yelps from our side of the fence were now met with a renewed sense of hostility. Rather than just a shaking fist and an empty threat of being tattled on. We were met with warranted verbal abuse and the threat of physical violence. This was fantastic.

Watching from the fence as the three players finished putting on the fourth green. You could tell that they were serious about their game. The back-and-forth chatter between the players was animated. As they drove the golfcarts up to the fifth tee box we could hear them hyping up for the next hole. Making eye contact with the leader of the group, his smile faded as he walked up the steps towards the tee. We were standing at the fence waiting with anticipation for the conflict that was about to unfold. The first player took his position. Placing the ball with delicate care onto the ground. Stepping back to adjust his stance, bouncing the weight of his body from foot to foot. Trying to get that perfect shot. The silence in the moment was heavy as everyone held their breath as the club was raised back. As the club approached the ball, right before impact, we shouted. The ball sliced in an unintended direction. The golfers all turned in our direction, as we fell over laughing. If looks could kill, there would have been a fatality. One of the men approached the fence to deliver us a warning about our tomfoolery. As he returned to his friends, we composed ourselves and returned to our spot along the fence. Watching the second player adjust his stance, address the ball and swing. With a crack, the ball launches off the tee. A great shot. Our anticipation building.

The leader of the group steps up for his turn. Dropping the ball onto the ground. Squaring up the shot. He stops looks back, over his shoulder at us. Not impressed but satisfied that we had heeded the warning. Our laughter was barely contained. Holding up my hands like I understood his warning and wouldn't dare make a peep on his swing. He turned back to address the ball. His stance widened; his attention focused onto the ball. His club raised, and the moment before impact we screeched. The ball launched to the left. Now this golfer was out for blood. His face was red, and fire burned from his eyes. He charged over to the fence, barking threats of bodily harm. We took a few steps back, putting some distance between us and the chain link. We started to chirp back with how terrible a golfer he is. His rage was building. Reaching over the fence trying to grab hold of our shirts or any other piece he could catch. We laughed and mocked his feeble attempt to get at us, and this must have struck a nerve. The golfer was now trying to climb over the chain link fence. It was only four feet tall and wouldn't take much effort to get over. This was the moment we were waiting for. The golfer's hands were on the top bar of the fence. His shoe was wedged into the diamond pattern of the chain link. He was coming over with rage in his heart. Chris charged at the fence, giving it a kick, knocking the golfer off the fence. I reached into the bush and grabbed the hose we had stashed. The golfer now stunned and sitting on the ground after being knocked off balance, was met with a blast of cold hose water. The steam that emitted from the golfer's body as he erupted into a Firey rage floated off into the air. His friends standing back in shock, with a look of amusement growing on their faces. They both backed out of range of the hose and started to chuckle. Standing back up and ready for war, the wet golfer, now shouting profanity and threats of death, charged back at the fence. I raised the hose and aimed it at the golfer. He was taking a full blast from the hose, while he tried once again to mantle the chain link. The back door of the house swung open. The bellowing shouts of an angry mother bursting into the yard.

"Hey, leave those kids alone!" The presence of an adult was enough to dissuade him from crossing into the yard. I put down the hose and climbed back down into the grass.

The golfer gave his final warning and an empty "If I would have got my hands on you!" statement and rejoined his golf buddies. As they drove off to continue their game you could hear them start to make fun of their wet companion. Chris' mom went back into the house and never mentioned anything about what she had just witnessed.

We continued to play in the yard, laughing and making noise. Not long after the wet golfer left, we had a visitor standing at the fence. "Hey, you kids," barked an old man standing on the golf course. "Were you hosing down golfers?"

We stopped playing and walked towards the man. "Who us, oh no, we are perfect little angels." I said with sarcasm. And we burst out laughing.

"Well, I better not catch you on this side of the fence, or your gonna regret it." The man said as he walked away. He must have told the wet player that he would do something about our shenanigans and gave us a warning. The old man was one of the course marshals. He spent the rest of the day, directing golfers from his position on the fifth hole. We stayed away from fence for the rest of the day, not wanting to press our luck.

Chapter 3: Gertrude & Friends

As the weeks went on, I was given my own responsibilities. I would start each day knowing exactly what objectives needed completing. One morning I had just finished filling the water coolers. I drove back into the shop to return the water trailer to the corner where it would sit until needed again. Unhooking the water trailer from the cart, I pulled the bolt from the hitch and wrapping the excess chain around the frame. Lifting the front of the frame and walking it back into its designated space. The almost empty water tank was easy to maneuver, the excess water sloshing around. When the water would slap the back of the tank the cart would lunge, and the frame would push back into my hands as the contained wave moved in the tank. After a few steps the water tank was tucked away safely. I was hungry and ready for a snack.

As I approached Lee's office, I could hear him in a conversation with someone. Lee was known to talk to himself, so I did not think much of it. When I got closer and could see through the window. I thought that he was alone. So, I stepped into his office to see if he had any specific tasks that needed to be completed. I stood in the doorway and found lee not to be alone after all. Standing in front of lee was a duck and her five ducklings. She was squawking at lee. The duck paid no attention to my arrival and continued to squawk. "Alright, see you tomorrow, Gertrude." Lee said to the duck. She gave a final quack and turned to leave the office. Gertrude and her five ducklings waddled past me without a care in the world, like I was not even there. They marched through the shop and out the back door.

I stepped into the office and took a seat in the chair below the window. There must have been a look of confusion on my face, as lee grinned at me. Lee then began to explain the interaction I had just witnessed. "That's Gerturde, she has been coming to visit me for the last few years.," He started. "She was just here to introduce the newest batch of ducklings." "They only hatched a few days ago." I smiled, impressed with his ability to communicate with the ducks. "I built them a little house last year, its just under my window here." Lee motioned to the window. "They have been nesting there ever since." I had noticed the wooden box outside, but never guessed it was a duck's nest. "It keeps the out of the elements, and they seem to like it." Lee continued "Gertrude was saying how happy she is with the accommodations." "She stops in every couple of days for a visit." I had a big smile on my face as lee told me about the ducks. I was happy that his Zen attitude was in tune with being one with the animals. "let's go for a ride.," Lee said, standing up from his chair. I went to the kitchen and grabbed a snack that I planned to eat as we traveled.

Lee and I got into his golf cart. it was always parked in front of his office door. The cart was not modified into a work cart, the straps to hold on golf bags were still attached to the back. His wife would take it out on the days she played. I rested my feet on the clean floorboards and instinctively look back as the cart moved backwards out of the shop. I didn't say anything as the cart drove towards the tunnel, just past the third green. On our trip around the course Lee told me stories of the past years. He had been the greenskeeper for over ten years and had seen a variety of people come and go. His stories gave me a strong sense of the history of the maintenance team. He had a few stories of the last lead hand ruling over the others with an iron fist. The story felt more like a cautionary tale than a funny anecdote.

One day Lee had returned from running errands offsite. He had been gone for an hour to get some overpriced replacement parts for one of the golf carts. Lee parked his truck and stepped out, holding the bag of parts he had just purchased. A faint mumble could be heard over the breeze, so he took a few steps forward to investigate. As he past the corner of the building he could see the cause of the noise. Lee started laughing as he approached the scene of the crime. The lead hand had been bound to the largest tree next to the wash station. His body was wrapped in silver duct tape. The multitude of wraps made it so he was unable to get free on his own. His body was hidden from the view of the golfers, the tree was wider than his thick shoulders. The others must have used an entire roll of tape to keep him pinned to the tree. He was a big and strong, it must have taken the whole team to pull off this level of mutiny. After being pinned to the tree he was blasted with the hose. The water pressure was not very high, but the fat hose blasted out an incredible volume of water. He was still dripping when walked closer. Lee leaned in and removed the cloth that had been used to gag the boy.

"What happened to you?" lee asked already knowing the answer.

"Cut me down!" he said angrily "I'm going to kill them all!" Lee took a step back and gave him a disappointed look.

"You haven't learned a lesson, while you have been waiting to be cut down?" Lee asked. Implying that the boy probably had this coming. Fire shot from the bound boy's eyes as only the thought of vengeance filled his mind. Lee took another step back and began to turn away.

"Hey, you can't leave me like this." The boy pleaded.

Lee looked back "You might need to hang there a bit longer, to figure a few things out." And continued into the shop to repair the broken cart. Lee returned to the tree to find the boy was more agreeable after having some time to reflect on his predicament.

As the tape was being cut the boy spoke "Yea, I guess I might have had that coming." He said with some humility in his voice. Lee said nothing and nodded in silent agreement. The boy finished out the remainder of the season, but never regained the respect of the others.

Lee's story still holds true today. You can't get peoples respect if fear and intimidation are your tools. Sooner or later a revolt is sure to take place. Lee was silent as he remembered back to that day, giving me a moment to have the story settle into my mind. As we passed the sixth green entering the shade of the concrete tunnel, Lee started another story. We exited the tunnel and Lee pointed out a patch of grass that was longer than the rest. Explaining that the long grass was an indication that there was a leak in the sprinkler line. The extra water causes the grass to thrive. Lee started to tell me the story of Jake.

Jake was a young man obsessed with his hair. His days were spent flipping his long hair out of his face. His emo bangs blocking his vision as he worked. Lee had sent him out towards the seventh hole to repair a blown-out rainbird sprinkler head. Jake had dug out the hole and removed the broken sprinkler. In the hole he found that the pipe had also split and needed to be fixed. He cut back the pipe, past the split in the plastic. He was planning on using a coupling attachment that would reattach to the sprinkler head. He uncapped the can of blue primer, leaning back into the hole to run the saturated dip stick over the exposed pipe. The thin blue liquid covering the pipe, with the excess dripping into the soil of the hole. He sat up and returned the applicator to the tin. Unscrewing the lid to the thick grey pipe glue. Leaning into the hole with the glue covered dip stick. Jake's Hair feathered into his eyes. With his left-hand providing support as he leaned into the hole, he used the back of his right hand to brush the hair out of his face. The glue applicator made quick contact with his head. The thick glue immediately locking into place. In a panic Jake pulled the applicator away from his head. A clump of hair stuck to the half-covered brush. His fingers probing as the spot, only to find a sticky mess. Upset, but with a task to complete, Jake leaned back into the hole. Hastily repairing the broken pipe, he reattached the sprinkler head. Tossing all the equipment into the back of his cart, he raced back to the shop. Lee was standing in the shop at the cart tires skidded to a stop outside. Jake rushed into the shop, heading straight for the bathroom. wanting to look in the mirror to check out the cranage. Moving past Lee, with his hand shielding the damage from view, he entered the bathroom. A plethora of profanity exited the bathroom. Jake gazed upon the large glue glob that was hardened into his hair. Lee stood in the shop, waiting for Jake to exit. After a few moments Jake exited the bathroom, his head held low, a look of defeat on his face.

Lee could see the giant glob of glue from across the shop, and sympathetically asked "What happened?" Jake told him the story and Lee held back a chuckle.

Jake went into the lunchroom to find a hat before the others could see him. Finding an old trucker style hat Jake finished out the day. Once the shift ended her rushed home and tried to wash out the rock-hard glue. The following morning Jake returned to work wearing a different hat. Entering the lunchroom with defeat still in his eyes. The boys in the lunchroom went quiet as he entered. All eyes were staring at Jake, wondering what was under the hat. Jake stared back; with sadness he removed the hat. The room erupted with laughter as Jake reveled his new buzz cut. The noise quickly died down and the room filled with supportive comments,

"It's only hair."

"It will grow back."

"It's not that bad."

"Wow you have a misshaped head." Some of the boys have more empathy than others. Walking out of the lunchroom past Lee, who had wandered by to see what all the noise was about. Lee getting a good look at the freshly shaven head, said nothing.

Lee chucked to me, as he pointed out the exact spot where the glue monster had attacked. Claiming the beautiful emo hair of Jake.

"This is a place for work, not a fashion show" Lee said. "Some days we are going to get dirty." I always wear my hat, so I was not to concerned about getting an unwanted hair cut. But my hair was getting long and starting to curl up, out of the back of my cap. The sun had been fading the patch of hair that was visible above the adjustment strap. We continued to tour the course, looking for fixable problems.

As we proceeded to travel around the course, Lee would veer off the paved path and park in the trees. Slowing down the cart as we seen the rabbits hopping into the bushes. We stopped and waited. The bunnies would then reveal themselves after a few minutes of silence. They would hop over in our direction. Lee would start to talk to them. He would natter away at the creature until it moved along to do whatever rabbits do. Then we would continue along. We made a few more stops to visit with the wandering animal creatures that inhabited the course. Until our journey ended, where it began, back at the shop. Lee parked the cart in the same first cart position, where it was always parked. It was already lunch time, so I joined the others in the lunchroom. I had spent some time with Lee over the following weeks and was not overly surprised that he was our local Doctor Dolittle. I had seen him out on the course over the past few the weeks, now it all made sense. Every time he was out pointing and flapping his arms, as if in a heated conversation. He was, but not with himself, like a crazy person. But as a crazy person talking to the local animals.

Chapter 4: Garbage & Tee Boxes

Collecting the garbage from around the course was the best of the weekend jobs, it was quick and easy. I would put on my Walkman and crank up the tunes. Starting at the first hole, working my way around the course. At each of the tee boxes the markers would also need to be moved. The markers were of two types. One being a wooden block, the other being a steel five-sided box with the top open, both styles had a spiked bottom. The open top was used to collect the broken golf tees. The players were expected not to leave the broken wooden tees littered across the tee box. Every other day the tee markers would be moved, either one step forward or one step back. They were not to be moved too far out of position as there were expectations that the distance to the hole would be consistent from one game to the next. If you moved them on Saturday, they would not need to be moved again until Monday.

After moving the markers, the garbage would be collected. The empty beer cans would be put into the back of the golf cart and the garbage would be dumped into a garbage bag. The further into the course, the more garbage you would collect. Each hole after the ninth would contain the unfinished snacks from the halfway house. The small amount of beer remaining at the bottom of the cans would attract the wasps. Each garbage can was potential hive. Collecting the garbage first thing in the day was a must, with the cool air keeping the wasps docile and moving slow. The collection of all the empty beer cans has ruined my ability to consume beer forever. To this day the smell of beer reminds me of stale hotdogs and dirty cans.

After returning to the maintenance building to throw away the garbage, the cans would be stacked neatly in carboard boxes. Once the boxes were stacked up to the roof, they would be returned to the recycle plant across the road. Transporting the empty cans was always tricky. If the boxes tipped over the cans would spill all over the concrete floor, making a huge amount of noise. The bottle depot liked when the cans were delivered in the boxes. It was a quick and easy to count, with each box holding twenty-four cans. Once all the garbage was disposed of and the cans stacked up in the corner, the work cart would be hosed out and returned into the shop. Having the cart washed down got rid of the lingering odors from the garbage and stale beer cans and kept the wasps away. Once the cart was washed and put away, the day was done, and I could go home and rest.

Chapter 5: End of Season

Most of the first season was spent walking the perimeter of the course carrying the gas-powered whipper. Knocking down the tall grass that sprouted on our side of the fence. Most days were spent patrolling the fence line, with headphones in, listening to the radio. The solitude was freeing, and the hours spent alone were therapeutic. Having the time to reflect inward on the future made the days go by quickly. The robotic nature of the perimeter march made losing yourself in deep thought easy. The hope of getting to use one of the ride-on mowers was fading as the summer days grew shorter. The time spent outside over the hot months were rewarding enough. I had made the decision to return the following year if they would have me. I was excited to get the raise and climb one more rung up the seniority ladder. Some of the older boys were not planning on coming back. They had put in their time at the course and were looking forward to university and the future beyond.

When the school year started, I was only able to work on the weekends. This was not terrible, as we only had to do the basic tasks on weekends. The workdays were short. I had worked most weekends over the summer and knew what to expect. I would get paid four hours regardless, even if the tasks took significantly less time. Filling the water coolers was quick, and so was collecting the garbage from the day before. Most weekends I would be back home in two or three hours.

Back in school, my dark tanned arms did not go unnoticed. The summer sun had turned my pasty white arms into a golden brown. I rolled up the sleeves on my shirt there was a distinct line where the tan stopped. When I had my shirt off, I looked like I was the recipient of a head and arm transplant. The extreme contrast between my dark neck and arms to my pale white chest was hilarious. I would tell anyone who asked, about how I had found a great summer job. Getting paid to be outside all summer was an easy sell. Not knowing at the time, that my words would pave the path for the seasons to come.

The golf season ended, and the course closed on the first of November. There were no more weekends to work. I waited patiently for the call to come back in the spring.

Chapter 6: Howling Tattoos

I was excited to start the second season. I had received the call that the course was going to open next week. I would be able to work on the weekends until school finished, then I would be full time. I was excited to get to work on the Monday after graduation. I had purchased a car before school year ended, a yellow Camero. I was excited to drive it to work. The alarm clock went off early and I got up with renewed enthusiasm for my employment. I got to the shop before anyone else arrived. I sat down in Lee's office, and we talked about nothing until the others started to arrive. Word had spread of the golf course being a great summer job, and we had in influx of applicants from my high school this year. I recognised a few of the faces as they walked in. We might not have known each other well at school, but the comradery of graduation was a strong foundation to build on. There were also students from across town who managed to find this job. It always seemed funny to me that peoples' jobs were never close to where they lived. If they were not from the neighbourhood they needed to commute across the city to get here. I guess I was lucky that way, I could roll out of bed and be at the course in five minutes, if I needed too.

One of the new workers that lived across town was a skater named Blain. He was a few years older than most of us. Blain thought he was cool. His long surfer hair floating behind him as he walked. The course had been open a few weeks, and we were starting to get to know how to test each others' boundaries. Monday morning rolled around; the summer air was warm. We were all sitting in the break room after finishing the first of the morning tasks when Blain walked in. He was quick to roll up his shirt sleeve to show off the new tattoo he got over the weekend. His skinny framed shoulder had now been decorated with a wolf howling at the moon encased in a perfect circle. The tattoo placement was immaculate, resting perfectly on his skin. Blain was somewhat of a unique hire, as Lee had some discriminatory hiring practices. Normally long hair, tattoos, piercings would be an instant disqualification. But Lee made the exception, even if past employees that met that description had soured future opportunities. When I asked Lee about why he felt that we he would say that they were unreliable, and lazy. He had enough people come through the door, so he was able to make a reasonable generalization based on a substantial sample size. And as the weeks went by, the reality of his negative stereotypes played out as he predicted.

The following Monday morning, Blain walked in wearing a tank top and his arm in a sling. He walked straight into Lee's office to explain his weekend injuries. Drew and I were already sitting in the chairs against the wall, under the window in Lee's office, waiting with curiosity to hear his tale of misadventure. It was a simple case of falling off his skateboard. As he reached out to break his fall he met the ground. The hard landing had dislocated his shoulder. The doctor had told him that he would be stuck in the sling for the rest of the season. Blain produced a doctors note to confirm the diagnosis. Lee told him that we had some light duties, and if he could manage, he was welcome to stay. As we all left the office to start the day, I took notice of Blaine's tattoo. Walking behind him, the wolf was looking right at me.

"Hey Blaine," I chirped "what's up with the tattoo?"

He stopped and turned around to face me. With sadness in his eyes, he explained "When I fell, my shoulder was dislocated, and the skin on my back shifted and relocated the tattoo."

It had moved probably three inches from its original perfect placement. Its final resting place was less than ideal, and now looked like it was placed without any care. He was not happy about this, but there was nothing that could be done about it. Blaine worked on his light duties for the rest of the day. Trying to push a mower or lift a whip was almost impossible. A few days of doing mindless tasks around the shop and Blaine, admitting defeat quit. The group was disappointed to see him go, but he lived across town and the time it took to get to the course was taking its toll. Blain made the best decision for himself, and no one would hold that against him.

Chapter 7: Rabbit Olympics

It was early in the season and the course was only open for a few days. A random spring snowfall made short work of the week. Drew and I were out on hole 15, working around the bridge. We had walked down into the channel to get a closer look at something that caught our attention from the elevated perspective of the bridge. We worked our way cautiously to the spot that we had seen from above. The ground was wet and slippery from the overnight flurry, so we paid extra attention to our footing. One wrong step and we would have slid down the hill into the unfrozen stream at the bottom. The ride down into the creek wouldn't be the worst part, the wet pants would be. As we got to the spot where the sparkle had caught our eyes. We found a broken club head shimmering in the light. Someone must have had a bad shot and had the club head fly off. I picked it up, and we started to climb up the hill. As we had moved to collect our treasure, we had wandered towards the fourteenth hole. We crawled our way up the steep incline. Drew was a few steps ahead of me. He got to the top and dropped onto his belly, motioning for me to do the same. I crept my way to the crest of the hill and looked down the fairway. I was expecting to see a deer, or a coyote standing in the fresh snow. The fairway was white, the overnight snow untouched and just beginning to melt. I scanned over the ground not seeing anything large on the horizon.

"Where?" I asked in a whisper.

Drew pointed silently to the right. My eyes locked on the rock trail the ran the length of the fairway. A culvert of rocks ran down the side, helping to direct the water overflow into the gulley. I then watched as a rabbit jumped over the rocks, kicking its legs apart doing a trick. I watched as it landed and ran back up the rock trail. It stopped and waited. There were six rabbits taking turns jumping over the rocks. Each one doing a kick or a twist as the pounced over the rocky gap. Then returning to the lineup to watch the others. We were being stealthy, watching the rabbits preform their tricks. We were there for a few minutes before we were interrupted by another worker driving down the cart path.

"Hey, what are you guys doing?" They loudly inquired from a distance.

The sudden burst of noise spooked the rabbits and the dispersed in different directions. The show was over. We got up off the ground and walked back towards our cart. Waiting next to our cart was the person with all the questions. We tried to explain what we had just witnessed, but they were not interested in the athletic achievements of rabbits. Their loss. I was always fascinated by the idea of wild animals playing games, and the way that they communicated with each other.

Chapter 8: Moving The Holes

Every other day the holes were required to be moved. As the holes were used, they would begin to lose their crisp edge. There were rules that needed to be followed when moving the holes. They needed to be moved far enough from their original position so that the old hole would not interfere with the new hole. They had to be far enough from the edge of the green so that they were not just next to the fringe. I would use the flag as a measuring stick, allowing me to get a standard reference of the hole positions. The flag was seven feet tall. Using it as a marker helped me to keep the distance from the edge of the green and the old hole consistent. Before I left the shop, I would load the cart with the equipment I would need. The hole cutting tool. A bucket, that was filled with some of the dirt and sand from previous holes. A pronged tool, used to fix the green if the grass around the hole was dented or damaged. A homemade hook tool, used to pull the cup from the ground. A flanged tool used to step the cup back into the ground at the regulation depth. I also brought along a twenty-litre gas jug that was filled with water. We had the jug marked with a giant "X" so that water was not mistakenly used as gasoline.

The hole moving process was quite simple. Remove the flag. Remove the cup from the hole. Locate the best spot for the new hole. Then using the lever action hole cutting tool dig a new hole. This tool was a wooden handle on a steel frame with a cup cutter on the bottom. There was handle in the middle that would push out the grass plug after it was cutout, just like an ice cream scoop. The steel cup cutter would be twisted into the ground, this would utilize your abdomen core muscles. The flange on top of the cup cutter guaranteed a perfect depth every time. Once the flange was resting on the grass you knew that the hole was the correct depth. I would do this in two steps first, I would twist until I felt the grass break free from the ground. Pulling out the core tool and using the side lever to drop the grass plug into the bucket. I would then return the tool back into the newly chosen hole. Giving the tool two or three good twists, while putting my body weight onto the handle, I could get out the rest of the dirt and sand reasonably easy. Once the flange was resting on the ground, with a satisfying pop sound, the tool would be removed from the earth. The tool would then be placed into the old hole, the lever would be lifted, and the collected dirt would fill the previous hole. The grass plug would then be removed from the bucket placed on top of the fresh dirt to close over the old hole. If the grass plug was not quite level, dirt from the bucket would be used to adjust the ground accordingly. The grass plug would then be stepped on to level it out and make a nice flat surface, matching the contour of the rest of the green. I would then water the plug to give it the best chance to regrow in its new location. The water jug would always start out heavy and as the holes were completed become more manageable. I would then place the cup into the newly formed hole and using the cup sinking tool with the large flange. Then Stepping on the tool to force the cup down to regulation depth.

There can be a few problems with not moving the correctly. Firstly, if the plug was not flush with the rest of the green, when the greens mower passes over that spot, the plug it would be scalped off, leaving a very noticeable circle of dirt. This was never a good thing, but the evidence would disappear in a few days as the short grass grows quickly. The next problem is if the new cup was not set in properly. By not being below the ground, golfers could hit the lip of the cup and have their balls not sink into the hole, costing them extra strokes. This would be deemed unacceptable, and the hole would need to be redone. There were always a few problems with the cups if they were not put into the ground straight or if they were not deep enough.

I always tried to place my holes within the limits of the regulations. My holes were not always in the dead center of the green. I always leaned them to one side. The week would start out with the hole on the left side, just past the seven-foot edge. Then I would move it to the back, keeping it close to the boundary. Then for the weekend I would place it just off the center mark. It was fun to keep the players guessing on where the holes were placed. The next week the holes might be closer to the front of the greens. Using the old plugs as markers, until they faded away, no two holes were ever in the same space on any given green.

However, the green on the thirteenth hole was a tricky situation. This green was one of the biggest on the course, and the hole distance was one of the shortest. The green had a two teer plateau that backed onto the neighbourhood street. The green was flanked on both sides by houses. The house on the left side sat below the grade of the ground. The top plateau of the green sat level with the gutters of its roof line. Whenever I cut a new hole on thirteen, the homeowner would come storming out. They would watch me and if I got anywhere close to the top half of the green, they would start barking complaints. I still needed to follow the rules for cutting holes on the green. But I would do my best to keep the hole to the lower portion. When placing each new hole, we would reach a compromise. I would place the new hole as close to plateau as possible. With them watching my every move. This led to some of my favorite hole placements. Sometimes hole would sit just off the cusp of the transition between the plateaus. Almost making it like a minigolf challenge. If the player under hit, the ball would roll back, costing them a stroke. I was not popular with the players on hole thirteen. The position of the house on the left was unfortunate. Anytime a player hooked a ball to the left it would bounce off their house. Previous years the stray shots had broken windows, plastic patio chairs, the glass on their patio table, even the lady of the house was hit while she gardened. So, they were always concerned with the flag placement. I did my best to trying and keep both the homeowners and golfers happy, but sometimes you can't be everything to everyone. Whenever I got hassled by a player about thirteen, I would just blame it on their game being terrible and not the placement of the hole. This was not the best strategy for customer service, but it got me out of the conversation quickly. I was not interested in their opinion on the placement of the hole, as it would always be at the top of the green. I wouldn't argue the placement regulations or the homeowners' concerns, I would just tell them to get better at their putts. And move on.

Chapter 9: The Net

Years before I started the course recognized that there was a problem on thirteen. The house on the left being was being struck by at least one player in every group. That house must have been hit a hundred times a day. The homeowner had started a collection of the golf balls that were pulled out of the back yard to prove the point. So, after the threat of legal action the course erected a giant net. The net was secured to three thirty-foot-tall posts. The posts were like the ones used to hold up the telephone lines. A cross brace was laid between them to fasten the top of the net, giving it some stability. The net was a great idea. It caught the majority of the hooked shots. But over time the net lost its tension, letting more shots through. The homeowners deemed to be unacceptable, so a repair was required. I was given the duty of fixing the problem. Not knowing how big of a task was at hand, I enlisted the help of Trevor and Drew. We loaded up the tallest ladder we had and went out to thirteen. I was early in the day; the morning frost was still on the ground as we arrived at the hole. We setup the ladder, leaning it against the post on the left. The ladder reached just past the top of the net. We spent the next few minutes arguing about who was going up the ladder to make the repairs. Drew and Trevor both claimed to have a fear of heights. I didn't believe this to be true, but I was nominated to make the climb. I don't have a fear of heights, I have a fear of falling. I was given the assurance that they would hold the ladder still, and that it's not a big deal. I started up the ladder, the morning air was cool, so I was wearing my work gloves. My back pocket was stuffed with zip ties, wanting to make this a quick repair. I got to the top of the net with three rungs still left on the ladder. I reached my arm over the cross brace to stabilize myself. I took a quick moment to enjoy the elevated view, not ever seeing the course from this vantage point. I could see over the trees and down the fairway of twelve. Taking one hand off the ladder, I reached back to collect a tie from my pocket. I got one and fished the plastic through the net. The satisfying clicks of the strap as it fastened the net back into place. When I reached back for the second strap that's when I felt the first tremor in the ladder.

"How's the weather up there?" the boys joked from the ground. I looked down to see them kicking at the feet of the ladder. I held on tight.

"Hey, don't you be doing that." I said with a hint of panic in my voice.

"No worries, we will hold the ladder still." They said reassuringly. Contrary to what they were actually doing. I gripped over the crossbar tightly. Taking off my glove and dropping it down on them.

"Don't you be shaking this ladder." I warned. I was starting to get warm as the blood pumped through my veins, my heartbeat pounding in my ears. I reached back into the net and pulled the second strap, locking it into place. I was able to reach six of the strap locations from the original ladder position. Once they were all secure, I started on my way down the ladder. When I got about halfway down the ladder, it began to wiggle again. Looking down at the boys as I descended, they had the look of a troublemakers. I stepped down quickly to the next rung, shrinking the potential fall distance. The closer I got to the ground the move the ladder swayed. When I had four rungs left, they stopped and stepped away from the ladder. With my feet safely on the ground, and a scowl on my face.

Trevor asks, "Why so serious?" As if he didn't know why.

Chapter 10: Always Cover Your Lips

It was almost lunch time. I was driving the golf cart back to the shop to collect the boys to go for a meal. It was Tuesday and we always went and got nuggets across the street. As I exited the tunnel dreaming of dipping sauce, a bee flew into my face. It felt like I got struck in the face by a stone. I raised my hand to smack it away, but it was stuck in my beard like a piece of Velcro. My hand contacting the large insect, knocking it away, but not before the bee stung me in the bottom lip. The point of impact was warm. Probing the location with my tongue, I could feel a hole where the stinger had struck. I pulled into the shop and told the boys what had happened, and they laughed. I had a small indent on my lip where the bee had zapped me. We went to get our nuggets, and I never gave it a second thought.

The next morning when I woke up, I went to the bathroom and caught a glimpse of myself in the mirror, my bottom lip was swollen. It looked like I got punched in the face. The bottom lip had swelled over night, the location of the bee's impact was clearly visible. I went upstairs and used the phone connected to the kitchen wall to call into work. Lee answered and told him that I would not be coming in. He did not have any questions, as he could hear the distress in my voice. My words were muffled by the engorged bottom lip. I hung up the phone knowing that I took the cowards way out by taking the day off. However, to avoid the relentless teasing that was sure to happen with my fat face, it seemed like the right move. The next day I was back to normal and other than telling the boys of my absence, never gave it a second thought.

A few weeks went by, and I had forgotten all about being sting in the lips. I left the house after supper and went for a short 20km bike ride. I was in shape and loved to ride my mountain bike through fish creek park. The deep valley was filled with wildlife and large trees. It felt as if you were in the mountains, but never needed to leave town. I had passed all types of animals in my previous travels, Deer, rabbits, a porcupine, I even seen a giant skunk once. There were snakes, gophers, and pheasants, those crazy little chicken birds would pop out in front of you as you passed the bushes. They would always give me a startle when the appeared out from the brush. I had just exited from under the overpass next to the garden center, I felt a familiar pinch in my lip. A bee had smashed into my face and stung me in the lip, again! In the exact same spot! It felt like I was pelted with a larger stone this time, as I was moving quickly down the path. It didn't hurt, but I immediately knew something was wrong and I needed to get home. My lip swelled up instantly. My whole body went into panic mode. I turned my bike around and peddled as fast as I could. As I passed other people on the trail, there eyes stretched big, filled with wonder and concern. My bottom lip was swelling up fast and had grown five times the size that it should have been. I peddled harder, moving faster, my lungs stretching to keep breath. My body began to itch. Every inch was on fire, a deep unyielding itch. My brain raced as it made the diagnostic calculations on survival and split into two options. My lizard brain was yelling to stop and roll on the ground to try and make the itching stop. The survival half of my brain was screaming that if you stop, you will die. So, I continued home with maximum haste, fighting the urge to roll in the dirt.

I made it back to the house in record time, dropping the bike on the front lawn. Racing up the front steps, I got to the front door and rang the bell multiple times as I went inside. Trying to make as much noise as possible to get my parents attention. I walked onto the front landing, stomping and shouting for help with an out of breath muffled voice. My mom appeared around the corner to see what the ruckus was about. There was an instant terror in her eyes.

I spoke out "bee sting." With a strange voice, as my tongue licked across my giant lip.

She ran to the kitchen, grabbed the car keys and we raced to the hospital.

We walked into emergency, and I went straight up to the check in desk and looked at the nurse. Her head was down as I approached. As she looked up to see what the problem was, with her robotic response at the ready, I said "bee sting."

Her eyes expanded wide as we looked at each other. She walked around the desk and grabbed my arm "right this way please." She had a sense of urgency but was not freaking out. I'm sure she had seen worse. She led me around the back, and I was put into a small room with a paper covered examination table and a wheeled chair. I sat on the table and the paper crinkled as I moved. She asked me to lay back, so I readjusted myself down the table, until I was laying down. She was looking in the cupboard next to the table and quickly found what was searching for. She sat on the chair and wheeled it into position. pulling my arm towards her, she poked me with an iv needle. Not giving me a moment to object. Then she attached a bag of liquid to the newly pierced hole and hung the bag above my head, to a metal stand that was next to the table. "This is an antihistamine." She explained this will counter act the bee poison and reduce the swelling. I could feel the clear liquid enter my veins, it felt like a cold stream rushing into my body. As it moved through my blood the itching started to subside and finally stopped. It was weird sensation to be aware of your own blood, but I could feel the pain disappear as the medicine flowed throughout my body. "Stay here, I will be back to check on you in awhile." She spoke. Leaving my mother and I alone in the room. I laid still and closed my eyes as the bag emptied.

"Well, I guess you don't have to wait if you get stung by a bee." I said. Trying to being some levity into the room. The truth of it was mom and I were both scared and in uncharted territory. I had never had a severe allergic reaction before and didn't know the protocol. About 20 minutes later the doctor arrived in the room to follow up on the situation. He attached a second bag of the medicine and said that when the bag was finished that the nurse would return to send me home. We thanked him for the quick service, and he left.

The nurse returned to check up on me. All the itchy tingles were gone, and my face was almost back to normal. My lip was still swollen slightly, but I was able to speak clearly again.

I thanked the nurse for the rapid response, and she said, "We don't mess around with allergic reactions, especially bee stings." She asked, "Have ever used an EpiPen or do you have one at home?"

I told her "No I don't, this was my first time needing one."

She explained how they worked and leaned in to show me how to use it. She Lifted my shirt and tried to pull some fat from below my ribs. She smiled as she told me "Normally this would be the spot, pinching the love handle and injecting the medicine, however you would not be unable to use that spot." "You don't have any extra meat on your bones, I suggest that if you ever needed to use the EpiPen to jab it into your thigh." I was in the best shape of my life and had only 2% body fat. I was still a walking skeleton, but I was wiry. I thanked her for the help and rested in the room for a bit longer. "You can stay in here as long as you need to" she said as she left the room.

We stayed a few more moments and then went home. The poison had been flushed from my body and I was feeling almost normal. We drove home quietly, we knew that today was a lucky day, and this could have gone way worse. Now every time I hear the buzz of a wasp or a bee, I cover my lips. To this day the expired EpiPen sits unused in the cupboard at moms' house. I'm sure my body would react more like the first time I was stung rather than the second. Only because of all the time that has passed between stings. I think the only reason I had the severe reaction to the second sting was because there was still poison in my veins from the first incident. But what do I know? I'm not a scientist, just an asshole that runs away from bees covering his lips.

Chapter 11: Pond Slime

There were three ponds around the course. These water hazards were a fantastic place to collect lost golf balls and birth hoards of mosquitoes. Resting in the ponds were home made fountains. The fountains were made from an old tire with a sprinkler mounted in the middle, they sprayed the water high into the air. The sprinkler helped to break the surface tension of the ponds, making it harder for the mosquitoes to nest. The fountains were be fueled by the irrigation system and needed to be turned on manually. A large hose ran from the sprinkler attachment to a water hatch located just to the edge of the pond. If the ponds were left unattended for a few days they would begin to grow a thick, slimy Algi that would create an unfavorable aroma for near by residence. We would often get complaints from the homeowners that the stink from the pond was so bad, that they were unable to enjoy their back yards.

My task for the day was to remove the slime from the ponds and put in a blue chemical to help remediate the future growth from the foul-smelling slime. I loaded the cart with some rakes, attached a grass clippings trailer, and went off to the first stop. There was a large pond behind the club house, so that was my starting point. It was always best to keep the most public areas tidy. This pond was directly behind the club house restaurant. It was flanked on the one end by a walking bridge that would take the players back to the parking lot after their game. The other end of the pond was the top side of a small waterfall and another foot bridge that crossed over towards the practice green. The water would overflow over the rocks and fall into the creek below. The sound of the steady flow of water over the rocks was soothing. The long edge of the pond ran along the edge of the restaurant patio.

I splashed the rake into the water, feeling the resistance of the slime as it rose out of the pond. The rake worked well enough at reaching the goop that was close to the edge. The rake however would not reach any of the slime that resided in the middle of the pond. I was limited by the length of my arms and the tools that I had. We were always told what to do, and not how to do it. I stood there for a few moments, contemplating a better solution. Cleaning the ponds was not a job anyone wanted to do. It was stinky and the smell of the slime always seemed to linger for days. After a few minutes I had an idea that might be the solution. Returning to the shop to get a rope, I planned out how to start the cleaning process. While I was at the shop, I found Drew and asked him if he wanted to come help me with the slime. He agreed and we returning to the pond. We stood in front of the water and stretched out the rope. I explained how I thought this solution might work. There was only one way to find out. I crossed over the bridge and stood on the far side of the pond, with my back to the patio, holding my end of the rope. Drew stayed on the other side. We pulled the rope taught and walked to the far end of the pond, keeping the rope out of the water. The rope starched across the pond easily as we had a long enough length. We dropped the rope into the water, next to the bridge, letting it sink into the goo. We waited for the rope to descend into the water then started walking slowly back towards the other parking lot bridge. The slime was collecting on the rope as we moved. Arriving back next to the bridge, I crossed over and pulled in the slime. Now we had most of the slime wrangled to a contained area. It was trapped in the containment of the rope. The slime would try and escape as we dropped the rakes into the water to fish out the goo. We stacked the slime into the greens clipping trailers. The excess water from the wet goop flowed out the back of the tail gate as the slime splashed into the container. We repeated the process with the a couple of times, making sure to remove all the unwanted green slime from the pond. Within an hour we had completed the first pond. There was not a single green floater left when we departed for the next location. We drove the trailer to the dumping grounds that were between the first and eighteenth fairways. The slime formed to the sides of the trailer and splashed out in a blob when we tipped the trailer. With the trailer emptied we continued on, leaving a trail of slime water marking our path.

The next pond was on the tenth hole. It was located to the right of the fairway. This pond was extra sour. It smelled like the bog of eternal stench. One of my friends lived in the house directly behind the pond. I would be reprimanded by his parents every time I made a visit for the state of the foul water. I was excited to use our newly crafted plan to clean up that mess. I wanted to make sure the course view they had was as pristine as possible. We departed the work cart and unravelled the wet rope. Each of us grabbing an end. And we walked to our respective sides of the pond. The rope trailing behind in the water collecting the slime as it pulled. This pond was just as easy as the first one. There were no obstructions on the oval shaped pond. The rope pulled the majority of the goop on the first pass. We dragged the slime onto the grass, straight out of the pond, then we filled the trailer with the goo using the rakes. Trying to stay out of the splash zone as the slime slurped into the trailer.

There was a new girl working at the halfway house and we wanted to get a closer look. Cleaning the pond took less time than expected, so we decided it was a good time to wander over and have a look. We planned to stop and have a cold drink at the snack shack once the pond was slime free. While I was working my way around the pond collecting the remaining slime I saw a fish. It was dead. Floating belly up in the pond. I called Drew over and we make a sneaky plan to give the new girl the fish. I pulled it out of the water and put it behind my back. We started to walk towards the snack gazebo. Stepping into the shade of the peaked roof we approached the counter. The expanded metal gate was open, and the new girl was working on some homework as we planned our order.

"May we please get 2 cans of soda, and a bottle of water." I asked.

She looked up from her work, not impressed with our presence. We had been making noise working in her area and it was hard to concentrate. She would be happy once we were on our way. We were both grinning, guilty smiles. She turned her back to open the cooler door. While her back was turned, I put the dead fish on the counter and waited. She turned back around and put the cans on the counter, next to the fish. Our hope of having her scream with fright over the sight of the dead fish were quickly dashed.

"Ahh, a dead fish, you got me." She said with zero enthusiasm. "I have brothers and have seen a dead fish before." She mocked. I grabbed the fish, and we paid for the soda and quickly left. Defeated in our childish attempt to giver her a fright. Her deflated response took all the fun out of it. I tossed the fish back into the pond and we walked back to our cart. Disappointed by the lack of results for our shenanigans. A playfully scared scream would have made the fish funny, but we got nothing.

As we were packing up to move to the final pond, Lee arrived to look over our work. Giving us the nod of approval at our results. He was impressed with the rope idea and the results it provided. Not knowing that we just tried to give the new girl a dead fish.

Chapter 12: Whippers

Mike and I were on whipper duty. I had left him on the last section of the 9th hole to go get more fuel for the whippers. They took a 50/50 mix of gas and oil to run the 2-stroke engines. I was driving back through the tunnel that went under the neighborhood street towards the tenth tee box. My eyes adjusting to the sunlight as I exited the cold, damp tunnel. I could see Mike walking the fence line, just past the tee box. I continued to drive the cart over towards him. I Parked the cart down the path just off the edge, out of the way of future golf shots. I grabbed the red fuel can with the x marked on the side. The big x was to distinguish it from the other gas cans, as to not mix up the fuels. Grabbing the whipper in my other hand I looked up to see how far Mike had moved along. As my eyes adjust to his position, I could see a homeowner charging towards the fence. The man seemed extremely agitated and was pulling a hose, blasting Mike with water. I dropped the whipper, and raced over to see if I could deescalate the situation. I expected there was some kind of dispute over the noise that was being made. We would have complaints often about the loud nature of our work. As I approached the fence, still holding the fuel can, I could see the look on Mike's face, and he was angry. This was an unprovoked attack and completely caught him off guard. Mike dropping his whip turned toward the fence to confront the homeowner.

"What the hell was that for?" he shouted. The homeowner lowering the hose as he also approached the fence.

"Hey, man are you alright?" he asked.

"No!" Mike continued to shout, "you just blasted me with the hose!" "What's your problem?" he asked, his voice returning to a natural level.

The homeowner still looking concerned responded with "I just saved your life."

Mike fired back with "How, did you think I was thirsty?"

The homeowner now with a squared-up shoulders and a puffed-up chest. "No, you were on fire!"

Mike and I looked at each other confused by this. Mike asked, "How do you figure that?" The homeowner pointing down to the discarded whipper on the grass.

"You were on fire." Mike reached down and picked up the whip, leaning it against the fence, with the motor resting at eye level.

"Holy cow, you weren't kidding!" he exclaimed. Looking at the back of the whipper motor, the plastic heat guard was melted and had scorch marks down the side. All the animosity Mike had melted away and was replaced with gratitude. "I didn't expect to have to say thank you to someone for blasting me with a hose but, thank you." Mike said. Still dripping from the water blast, he had just received. I was standing there surprised at the situation.

After quickly inspecting the back end of the whipper, "It looks like the fuel hose came loose, sending fuel onto the hot manifold." I explained. "That would probably do it," I finished. The whip was in bad shape, the whole side was melted. "This could have been way worse." I stated.

"Thanks captain obvious" Mike said with some irritation back in his voice. The realization of what could have been creeping into his mind. Thanking his unexpected savior again, we packed up the whippers, got in the cart and started back to the shop. On the way back we started to joke about the situation.

"When I saw you get hosed, I was ready to jump the fence and fight that old guy." I said jokingly. Mike smiled and shook his head knowing that was never going to happen. Arriving back at the shop Mike unloaded his destroyed whipper, taking it over to the work bench. Doug was there working on another project.

"What did you break it this time?" Doug scolded.

"We had a fire" Mike responded unenthusiastically. Doug looked surprised as the melted whip hit the bench. The melted plastic guard looked disgusting sitting on the steel work bench. It sat there for a few days as a reminder of what could happen. We all made it a point to double check the fuel lines on the whips just to make sure this malfunction was not repeated.

Chapter 13: Maximum Max

Deep in the unplayable space between holes was a mystical location. A giant tree provided shade to the forbidden zone, it was always dark and cool. A great place to hide from the summer heat. Within that boundary between the 7th and 8th holes lived a giant beast. Behind a barrier of a chain link fence, that divided the course territory from the residence, he lurked. Waiting patiently to strike as any unsuspecting prey wandered into his domain. Walking into the shade with the grass whip spinning loudly, I had not noticed that I wandered into the forbidden territory. Looking up just in time to see huge teeth appear out from the darkness. Maintaining my balance and regaining composure, I turned off the small motor. The fresh silence was broken by a deep howl of a bark. I looked through the chain link and there it was. The beast of eight. This giant bear of a dog with his paws draped over the four-foot fence. Barking out for attention. This was Max the dog a Newfoundlander breed. His curly jet-black fur was thick and made for the perfect camouflage in the always shaded darkness. Max took great pleasure in charging the fence to give a startle as anyone approached. He spent everyday in the yard waiting for his opportunities. He would pace the fence line as you trimmed the grass in front of his home. Max was not a vicious dog by any measure, but his size made him extremely intimidating, and most people would give him lots of space. Walking up to the fence, calling his name, Max calmed down and the barking stopped. I continued to trim the grass along the fence and went on about the day.

The following day I was working around the pond that was under the giant trees shaded radius. In the distance I could see Max pacing in the yard. Waiting for the chance to let out a bellow to raise my heartrate. As I worked my way around the pond, closing the distance between us. We made eye contact. Max sprung into action and charged toward the fence, barking with his giant teeth visible. Normally max would get to the fence and just drop his paws over the edge. Standing tall and looking even more humongous. On this occasion his excitement was overwhelming, and his massive body cleared the fence. As this monster jumped the fence, my stomach sank. Our eyes met as his paws landed. The look of panic in his eyes were met with the same expression coming from my direction. We had always had a barrier between us. I was always told he was friendly, I guess today we would find out if that was true. Max was not happy about being outside the safety of his yard. He backed up towards the fence that he jumped over with extreme ease. Realistically the fence was only a token measure to keep him contained, at any point he could have pounced over it without any real challenge. But today he had, in with an unplanned escape. He pressed his thick fur up against the chain link, hoping that his body would melt trough the fence and back to the safety of his home.

I put down my tools. Raising my hands, palms out, and started to approach the speaking to Max as I approached. Providing reassurance and encouragement of the safe return to his home. Max was visibly upset, his giant form trembling against the fence. His normal giant bravado diminished to a scared tiny creature. He had never been on this side of the fence and was not happy about it. As I got closer to Max and he did not move. He was looking at me with his big sad eyes. I reached out slowly and touched the top of his head, talking the whole time. His soft curly fur pressed back into my hand. His vicious facade melted away and all that was left was a friendly dog that wanted to get home. The fences that lined the course did not have any gates that opened into the grounds, so we would need to walk around. I had the keys to open the maintenance gates that bordered onto the street. Lost in his thick fur was a collar. I reached my fingers in between the curls and took hold. I looked up and counted the houses from the corner to where max lived. Five houses from the end. I told him that I was taking him home and gave a little tug on the collar. He was apprehensive to leave the comfort of being pressed up to the familiar fence. With some reassurance and a heavy pull on the collar I got him moving. We walked along the fence line and made our way to the street. I unlocked the gate. Once we were on the sidewalk max was filled with a new invigoration, he recognized the surroundings. He must have taken this street hundreds of times while on walks with his family. I counted the houses as we walked. Apon reaching max's house, we walked up to the front door. I pressed the button and the doorbell rang with a melodic chime. I could hear a shuffle from behind the door, the latch clicked, and the door opened slowly. A surprised lady appeared, shocked by the arrival of her dog.

"Max, jumped the fence." I told her.

"Well, he has never done that before." She claimed. Max was happy to be home his tail wagging, pulling to enter the house. I leg go of his collar and he walked into the home. He almost knocked over the lady in the doorway with his massive body. She thanked me for his safe return and closed the door. I walked down the street, returning to the maintenance gate. I locked the gate and went back to work. Max was already back in the yard. With his paws draped over the fence watching the world from the safety of his yard.

Chapter 14: Lost and Found

Paul was with us for a while. He lived with Drew and they both had second jobs at the grocery store. After working all day at the course Paul would walk over to the store from the maintenance building. It was as short distance; you could see the grocery store from the edge of the course. The neighborhood was still being developed, and there were a few businesses in the strip mall along the way to the grocery store. One of the larger businesses being a vehicle repair shop. As Paul strolled down the edge of the parking lot, something shiny caught his eye. As he got closer to the shimmer, he could see a set of keys on the warm pavement. Looking around as he approached, he bent down and collected them. In 1999, vehicles had just stated to have buttons put onto the ignition keys. He pressed the button and was greeted with a small honk. Looking around, he pressed the button again, this time seeing lights blink as the horn chirped. He continued onto work, placing the keys into his pocket.

Over the next few hours Paul struggled on what to do with the keys. After his shift had finished, he walked back over to the vehicle. His hand gripping the keys tightly inside his pocket. He pressed the button, and the lights blinked as the doors unlocked.

Temptation got the best of him, and he opened the car door. Might as well see if the car starts, he though. The key trembled as it entered the ignition. With the slightest turn, the engine roared to life.

Saturday morning as I fueled up the maintenance cart I was using, I could hear a rumble off in the distance. As the growl grew closer, I looked up to see who was coming down the shop's driveway. A white sports car approached, parking next to my car. The engine shut off and the morning piece and quite returned. The car door opened a Paul got out, grinning with excitement for his new toy. I walked over to admire the newly acquired transportation.

It was a white, convertible 1999 chevy Camaro SS. The giant hood scoop steamed hot air into the cool morning.

"Do you like my new car?" he asked with excitement.

"I sure do," I said pointing over to my 1987 yellow Camaro, "the new ones look great."

Paul nodded and walked off into the shop to start his day, and I went to start mine. I didn't give too much thought into where the car had come from, we were all working and maybe he got a car loan. That's what I had to do to get my $1200 yellow Camaro.

Weeks had passed and Paul was still driving the car to work. It was always clean, not a spec of dirt anywhere. Paul was keeping his ride spotless almost to the point of obsession. As time passed no one expected anything to be out of the ordinary with regards to his vehicle.

One hot summer evening Paul was cruising around in the Camero, top down, enjoying the cool breeze. Pulling into the local gas station for some fuel and snacks. On the way back to his car, a couple of teenagers were checking it out.

"Hey man, nice car" the one stated excitedly. "Would you ever want to sell it?" asking with hopefulness.

Paul took a quick second to think about it. "Sure, I would." Paul said. "If you follow me home you can take it for a test drive to see if you like it." Paul suggested. "We can work out a price, if you do."

The teens were excited and agreed to follow him home. Paul parked the car out front of the house, and the teens pulled in behind him. The one got out and walked over saying "My dad will be happy we found such a sweet ride." They traded car keys as a form of collateral, then the teens jumped into the Camero. The ignition fired up, and the car vibrated with the satisfying rumble of three hundred twenty-five horsepower. They pulled out cautiously, turning at the corner to get back on the main street of the neighborhood. Once they were on the divided road the car roared to life as they stomped down on the gas peddle. The Camero increasing speed incredible fast, the engine rumble disappearing into the night.

Paul waited a few minutes outside in the front yard, then went into the house to hand out the snacks that were purchased from the gas station. He wandered through the house delivering the treats and talking with the other roommates. A fair bit of time had passed. Paul, walking into the kitchen to check out the time on the microwave. The digital numbers showing that the teens have been gone for almost an hour. He still had their keys and was not overly concerned about their return, expecting it to be at any moment.

The warm summer night was calm and silent until the front door of the house was forcefully opened with a boot. The back door was also kicked in at the same time. Rushing into the house through the front and back doors with weapons drawn were the police. With a coordinated entry the cops breached both doors at the same time. A whole squadron of fully geared up tactical members of the Calgary police force marched into the house.

Shouts of "hands up, don't move!" rang throughout the house.

The police were met with zero resistance, and everyone was instructed to get into the front room. It was the largest room in the house. Some of the boys sat on the sofa, with their hands on their knees not daring to move.

"Who drives the Camero?" one of the officers asked sternly. A few eyes looked over in Paul's direction.

Paul reluctantly raised his hand, "I do, sir." He said sheepishly.

"You're going to have to come with us son" the first officer replied. As a second officer placing his hand on Paul's shoulder directing him out the front door. Paul and the officers walked out to the front yard. As the rest of the tac team surveyed the area and made their way out of the house.

One officer turned and said, "The rest of you stay out of trouble, or we will be back." The boys in the front room looking at each other with wide eyes and raising pulses, surprised at what just happened in the last five minutes. No one said anything for awhile.

Outside Paul was being escorted towards one of the police cruisers that now lined the street in front of the house. there were four cop cars on the street all parked at different angles. Once Paul reached the car the officer opened the door and instructed the teenagers in the back seat to exit the vehicle. The teens were pale and looked at Paul with contempt.

"Is this the person that gave you the car?" the officer asked.

"Yes, sir" the teens answered one after another.

"Do you have their keys" the officer directed the question to Paul.

"Yes, I do sir. In my pocket." Paul said.

"Give them the keys" the officer instructed. Paul reached into his pocket, pulled out the car keys and handed them to the closet teen. The officer let out a sigh "Alright, you two can go, but I better not catch you out here again."

"Yes sir, thank you sir." The teens said gratefully as they trotted back to their vehicle and left quickly, before the officer could change his mind.

"So, why are you trying to sell a stolen car?" the officer inquired. Paul said nothing. "We caught those two speeding a few blocks from here." The officer explained. "After pulling them over and running the plate, low and behold, the car comes up as stolen." "As I'm asking them questions about their involvement with the stolen car and explaining the trouble they were in." "They tell me, they are test driving it for a possible future purchase and had no idea that it was stolen." "The fear and confusion on their faces led me believing that they were telling me the truth." "So, I asked where they got it, and they brought us here, to your house." "So, why are you trying to sell as stolen car?" the officer asked again.

Paul clearing his throat began to answer, "I thought I could get rid of it, sir."

"How do you mean?" the officer asked.

Paul continued "I have had the car for awhile and thought this might be a good opportunity to get rid of it."

The officer thanked Paul for his honesty. "I'm going to have to place you under arrest." The officer explained "and we are going down to the station for some paperwork." The officer pulled out his hand cuffs and instructed Paul to turn around as he put them on. Paul was then placed into the police car and taken to the neighbourhood police station.

The boys back in the house with their faces pressed against the front window watched as Paul was put into the police car and driven away. The room erupted with speculation to the cause of the night's events, as the police cars drove away from the house.

As the sun started to come up Paul walked back into the house. His fingers freshly stained with ink from the booking process. He went straight to his room and fell into bed. Paul did not get a chance to have much rest as the house was a buzz over the previous nights police raid. Paul, giving up on sleep, walked into the front room where he had some explaining to do. He told his story of finding the keys, taking the car, and letting the kids take it for a drive. The other boys told him how bad of an idea it was, and then as boys do, told him all the ways they would have done it differently as to not have been caught. As the conversation turned back to what was going to happen next. Paul explained that he would have to go to court and see what the punishment would be. Until that time if he stayed out of trouble things would not get any worse.

As Paul's day in court quickly approached, he started to get nervous. Having never been in this situation, his mind started to playout all the worst possible consequences. The law was tough, and you could spend two years less a day in jail for stealing a car. That grim reality never crossed his mind as he plucked the keys from the ground months ago. When the day in court finally arrived Paul walked into the courtroom, shoulders back, head up, ready for whatever was about to transpire. He was ready to face the consequences for his actions. He stood there, quietly waiting for the judge to render the punishment. The judge looking directly at him, cleared her throat and said, "After looking over this case, and seeing that this is your first time before this court, and taking into consideration that the vehicle in question was not vandalized or in any other way recklessly damaged." She took a breath "It is this courts ruling that you will receive a conditional discharge and a five hundred dollar fine." Her gavel banging on the desk. Paul let out a sigh of relief and thanked the judge. His expectations were that he was going to have to send some time in jail. Only having to pay a fine was fantastic news. The guilt and worry he felt over the potential outcome of this hearing was punishing enough, and he had learned his lesson.

Chapter 15: Fairway Mower

Cutting the fairways was my favorite task. The machine was the biggest in the fleet. It had two giant tires in the front and two small tires in the back. When I turned the steering wheel the two tires in the back would move, giving this machine a tight turning radius. There was a joystick on the right-hand side that would drop and lift the cutting reels. Forward to drop, back to raise. It would take all day for me to cut all the fairways. The fairways were the largest section of grass on each of the holes, they filled the space between the tee box and the green. Looking out from the tee box towards the green the goal was to cut the grass in a crosscut pattern. This crisp argyle pattern would give the players a fantastic looking approach towards the green. After all the lines were cut, as a clean up, I would go around the outside edge to catch all the spots that might have been missed from lifting the reels early. I did not have to worry about pulling a trailer as none of the grass clippings needed to be collected, they would just disappear back into the grass and disappeared. This monstrous machine took the purple gas, Deisel fuel. The machine's fuel tank would need to be filled up twice a day, and running out of gas was never an option. If I did run out of diesel, the fuel lines would need to be bled to get all the air out of the system. Doug, our mechanic would not be impressed if he had to leave his work bench and venture out of the shop to fix such a preventable situation.

Each fairway I would start with a single stripe that would set the tone for how the grass would be cut. I didn't want to start with a line that was too long, or the finished cut would be crooked. The machine would keep straight lines fairly well. However, if I got over ambitious and tried to make the stripes too long the cuts would wonder, making the fairway look like a candy cane. The repetition of dropping the reels then raising them as I approached the edge of the fringe was a good exercise in focus. I had to pay attention, the joystick was delayed slightly, raising the reels moments after it was pulled back. This was a hydraulic function and did not have an immediate response to the controls. Behind the joystick was a built-in glove box. The cover had disappeared long before I started working at the course. In the box I would keep a drink and my radio.

This unit only had two speeds, slow, for cutting the grass, and medium for moving between the holes. The top speed could not have been more that about 10km an hour. Once I cranked up the speed to the fast setting the machine would bounce along the turf. The cart paths were not quite wide enough to accommodate the width of the massive front tires. The rubber would ride over the edge of the path, touching grass on both sides. As I was moving from hole number one past the tee box on the second hole. The machine transitioned from the grass to the broken cart path. Bouncing down the path with the radio in my ears. A new song from Smashmouth, started to play. I took my eyes from the path to turn up the radios volume. With "all star" blasting in my ears, the front left tire bounced into one of the boulders that was used as a retaining wall to elevate the second tee box. The mower was then twisted as it bounced to the right. Striking the back right tire into the curb of the cart path. I stopped the machine and got out to survey the damage. The back tire had fallen off the mower and laid flat on the ground. My mind raced and filled with the anticipation of the anger I would soon have to face. I started to walk back the short distance to the shop to get some assistance.

Inside the shop I found Lee. He was just about ready to go make his first rounds of the day. Every few hours would tour the course checking to make sure everyone was doing what they were supposed to be doing. Sometimes he would drive around in his golf cart, other times he would drive by in his green truck and investigate the course from the street. He always had an eagle eye on what was happening. If you thought for a second you could pull a fast one, you would be wrong. He knew everything. Lee was just about to leave on the golf cart as I approached.

"Lee," I said sheepishly "I had an accident."

Lee looked up from his cart and asked "did you crap your pants."

"No, I did not" I told him. Then clarified my predicament and told him "I crashed the fairway mower into the second tee box."

"Get in, let's go take a look" he said calmly. I was instructed into the golf cart, and we would go inspect the damage together. We quickly returned to the broken mower to find it exactly how

I left it. Crooked on the path, with a tire broken off resting on the ground.

Lee took a moment and inspected the damage. Lee said nothing. I start to explain how such a thing could happen, with expectation of getting blasted with a shot of anger. And a sermon on care and responsibility. Lee said nothing. He motioned back to the cart. I got in and we went back to the shop. Lee said nothing. That silence was the worst punishment that could have been handed out. I knew that I had messed up. I knew that I didn't use the concentration and care required to operate that machine. I knew he was not happy about it. But Lee said nothing. Back at the shop we gathered a tow rope and took the green gator back to the crash scene. Lee attached the tow rope; I got back into the mower and was pulled back to the shop. Lee said nothing.

Our second arrival was met by the others as it was snack time. Doug the mechanic looked on as we pulled into the shop. He was less than impressed as he now had a major repair to undertake. With my head hung low the others walked past the wreckage. After Doug's post snack inspection, it was found out that I actually did quite a number on that machine. The rear wheel had broken off and the bolts that hold it in place were sheared from the mounting rotor. This would be an expensive fix. And Lee said nothing.

It took a few days to get the mower up and running. Once the wheel was reattached it was ready to go. Doug had sent a few days putting it back together, taking his time, making sure the repair would last. As I was standing in front of the machine in awe of its massive size Lee approached.

"I'm sure you will be more careful this time." He said with a slight level of sternness.

"I absolutely will." I said with a renewed commitment to concentration.

"Good" he said "I'm sure you will.

"Why did you not get mad at me for breaking the machine?" I asked, using this moment to get some answers on the silent treatment.

"What good would that have done? He asked rhetorically. "The damage was already done, and I'm sure you knew the mistake." "Getting mad would not solve anything." "Now if this happens again, we will have a different conversation."

"Thanks for that, but the silent treatment was killing me, I expected some fireworks." I said.

"I know, and that's why you will remember to be more careful in the future." Lee explained

Of course he was right. I took more away from the silence that I would have from a loud exchange of angry words. I nodded in acceptance and stepped up into the mower, ready to take the first stripe in the road to redemption. Lee turned and walked back into the shop as I drove towards the first fairway. I was ready to prove that I was still capable of taking care of the fairways. As I made my way around, I passed the spot where I had mashed up the mower the week before. Learning from my mistake I stayed on the grass and did not try to thread the needle between the rocks and path curb ever again. Whenever we would have a new pilot of the fairway mower, I would make mention of that specific pitfall and suggest the grass as the best path forward. Passing on the knowledge so someone else could learn from my mistake and not cause another costly repair.

Chapter 16: Rough Mower

The perimeter of the course was the longest grass on the course. We called it the rough. It was not quite out of bounds, but if the players wandered in this wasteland, they might not find their balls with ease. This section of grass was managed by a large mower with a single deck that would cut an eight-foot swath of the overgrown turf with ease. There was a lever on the right to maneuver the deck, forward to drop, back to lift. If I moved the handle forward too quickly the mover deck would slam onto the ground, so a bit of finesse was required, to keep the machine moving smoothly. This mower was designed to get into all the hard-to-reach places. It had a reasonably tight turning radius and was great for going around all the trees. Any of the missed grass from around the trunks would be easily cleaned up by one of the other workers running the whips. The rough area was exactly that, rough. The ground had sprouted grass all-over the uneven earth, leaving hundreds of unseeable hazards. Moving through the longer grass, the blades would clang loudly if a stray stone found its way into its the path. Not small rocks, but stones protruded from the ground, unseen but felt as the mower passed over. Golf balls with their bouncy characteristics would shoot out the side of the deck, becoming unwanted projectiles, when they were passed over. The shrapnel from an exploded golf ball would disperse among the grass clippings, never to be played again. With the grass being cut to a uniformed level, the dips and holes hiding below were almost undetectable. Making the rough an easy zone for the golfers lose a ball and add precious strokes to their score card. After a few trips around the course, I became familiar with the low spots and the larger of the stones.

Cutting the grass on hills was the true test of nerves. The angled slope of the hill determined how much of a risk was worth taking. The mower was completely safe and the risk of tipping over was minimum. A slope would need to be over a forty-five-degree angle to actually roll over and none of the hills on the course met that requirement. But when mowing the hills the feeling that I was pushing that limit was ever present. The feeling of danger was invigorating as I slowly drove the mower down the edge of the channel. The mower deck had no flexibility, so I needed to commit to the move. Mowing the ridge parallel to the water was the only option. If I drove the mower straight down the hill the momentum would get me stuck in the mudbank at the bottom. The mower also did not have the traction required to drive back up the hill backwards, so I could not make it back up the hill if I went headfirst. The first run was always easy, I would make it to the end of the channel and turn back up the hill. Finding a flat open space on the fairway to make a U-turn. I reapproached the channel ready to drive deeper down the hill for a second pass. The further down the hill I went the more caution was required. As I made the final decent down the hill, after seven successful runs, the mower started sliding down with the freshly cut grass causing the tires to slip. The rear tire dropped off the edge into the mudbank. I Pressed the accelerator trying to give the mower even more forward momentum, hoping to straiten out and have the rear wheel slide back on the solid ground. With no luck, the mud gripped the tire firmly, pulling the mower deeper into the sludge. The ridged nature of the machine pulling the front drive tire over the bank and splashing into the creek. The tires spun, sinking deeper into the soft, muddy ground, launching the wet dirt into the sky. The stink of the sour water started to fill the air. I was officially stuck. It would be a long shameful walk back to the shop to get some assistance to pull the mower out of the mud and back up the hill. Admitting defeat, I climbed to the top of the hill and started the journey to get help. Not too far down the path I could see one of the other workers with a golf cart, so I changed my destination and went over towards them. They took me back to the shop with a bit of teasing and dropped me off, then they returned to their original location to finish whatever I had interrupted.

Walking into the shop, I was immediately teased again for getting stuck. Once the verbal pokes were finished, Lee and I got into the green's topper machine. This was a special day. The topper was not used very often. It had a very specific use and did not have any other reason to be taken out. Other than the occasional tow.

The toppers' primary function was to evenly distribute sand onto the greens after they had been aerated. It had a vertical brush with stiff bristles on the back that would spin, dropping the sand out onto the greens evenly. It was also the only machine that had a manual transmission. This made it good for pulling out stuck equipment, as you could utilize the low gears for better traction control. I rode as a passenger as Lee was extremely protective over this unit. I gripped onto the side handle as we moved towards the channel. The seats on the topper were in perfect condition, there was no tape required to keep them together. The milage of the unit was counted in hours and was still under five hundred. The center of gravity on the machine was strange, the seats were forward and rested over the front tires. This gave the illusion of nosediving as the machine drove over some rougher terrain. Lee pulled the topper in front of the ridge where the rough mower waited below. The one side of the mower was covered with the splattered mud from my unsuccessful self recovery attempts. I was handed a strap and walked carefully down the hill towards the water. I strapped it on the front, just above the mower deck and climbed into the driver seat, turning it on. I waived up to Lee to start pulling. The mower, being pulled slowly, started to twist out of the mud. As the mower straightened out and started being pulled up the hill, I made sure to steer the rear tires to keep the machine in line. Reaching the top, I was pulled a few extra feet onto the safety of the flat ground. I jumped off the mower, unhooked the strap, and returned it to the topper. I was given a few words of encouragement and a warning to not come back stuck again, at least for a little while. Getting stuck was just part of the job, it happened often so there was no real trouble to be had. Some of us learned quicker than others where the trouble spots were, doing our best to avoid them.

The holder of the record for the most "I got stuck" moments in a single day was held by the Silver Fox. He was on the rough mower and decided to clean up the creek edge by the shop. It was not a steep hill, but the bank was uneven and didn't have a consistent edge. He managed to get stuck a crushing 14 times before lunch. He would mow, get stuck, get retrieved, move forward a few lengths of the mower and the tire would drop back into the soft bank. This repeated for the whole morning. After the first couple of times, he was given a buddy to help, just to make sure he was safe. It took him the whole day to finish the entire creek edge, but when it was complete it looked fantastic.

Chapter 17: Greens Mower

Cutting the greens was the most prestigious role to be given out. It held the most responsibility. Every player would see how good or terrible that the job was done. Cutting the greens had the same design as cutting the fairways. Starting with a straight base line, then with minimal crossover returning over the green to give the grass a proper two-tone finish. Cutting the greens while they were covered with a morning dew made the job easier, as you could see where you had cut by the disbursement of the moisture. Cutting the greens quickly and efficiently was important. The golfers would start half an hour after the mower was fired up. It was a daily race to see if the players would catch up. On some occasions when the players were aggressively quick, they would have to wait for a green to be completed before they were able play through. Normally in that situation I would hold back on the next hole and let them play through the next hole. This would provide a nice buffer and relieve the tension of being chased by the players. Golf being a game of concentration it was a fair curtesy to give the players some space. The course had a special permit to operate the machines early in the day. The first two holes didn't have any homes near enough to complain about the predawn noise. The third hole however had a couple of houses that neighbored the third green. The way the homes were situated on their lots, they ran parallel to the fence. The green was only thirty feet from the side of the homes. If the first two greens were cut too quickly, then I would arrive at the third green before the permits were activated. I would need to skip the third green and return after cutting the seventeenth hole. This was never an ideal option as you would then be going against the flow of golfers, and they were never pleased if they needed to wait for the interruption. When the third green was cut early in the day and if the neighbours were woken from their slumber, we would get an angry complaint.

The whole task of cutting all the greens would take around four hours. It was a consistent job and there was not much room for making up any time. The greens mower would pull around the small trailer to collect all the fresh clippings. When the tailer was getting full, I would waive over one of the others so that they could take it away too be emptied. They would race to the dumping grounds and try to return before the next green was completed. In the middle of the season when the grass grows extremely fast, we would make a plan in the morning to have one of the other teams drop off a second trailer at the ninth hole. I would trade the full trailer for the empty one, returning later to retrieve it.

As I traveled down the twelfth hole fairway, I could see it there, in the middle of the green. Waiting for a rematch from the day before. I took a big breath and let out a sigh. Here we go again I thought. I approached the green with caution, dropping the trailer next to the cart path. Planning out my line of attack.

The beady eyes never looking away from my direction. I turned the mower towards the green and approached slowly. I cut the first stripe, then the second. No problems yet. On the third stripe I could reach the flag, pulling it from the hole without getting off the mower. I tossed the flag towards the clippings trailer. The flag flies like a javelin hitting its mark, the cloth clapping in the wind on its short journey. As I turn to make the fourth stripe, I knew the conflict was about to begin. Sitting in the path of the mower was a Canadian goose. This stubborn creature was going to stand its ground, refusing to give up his territory. This oversized ivory feathered menace had absolutely no fear of the mower, or of me for that matter. Our eyes met and I knew I was in for a battle of wills. I have a job to do, so I move slowly forward towards him. He does not budge. I don't stop moving. With a flap of disapproval, the goose is pushed to the edge of the green. The grass collection buckets protected the goose from the spinning reels and made for a good battering ram. I raise the reels at the greens edge and turned the mower to make the next cut. The goose runs back to his space with his wings extended and takes a defensive stance. I approach his adjusted position, and the mower pushes him again, to the other side of the green. Once the goose is off the green, it turns and runs back to his original spot, this time with his head down to obtain extra speed. The following stripe was outside of where he was standing. As the mower passes by the goose lets out a defiant hiss, claiming its victory over the defended territory. I finished the green, the goose never breaking eye contact with me on the mower. I drove over to the cart path and hopped off the mower to dump the clippings and retrieve the flag. I walked over to the hole, holding the flag straight up, trying to be as least combative as possible. The hole was not directly in front of the goose, so entering his space was unnecessary. As I placed the flag the goose honked, spreading out its wings in a show of force. I walked backwards to the mower not breaking sight with the goose.

"Well played goose" I said as I climbed onto the mower. "See you tomorrow." And I drove off to the next green. I laughed to myself; how often do you get to play chicken with a goose?

Chapter 18: The Lucky Tunnel

I never understood why someone would vandalise a golf course. It happed far too often. Sometimes it was just some idiot smashing up the green with the cart path indicator signs. Their steel construction would leave deep grooves and scars on the green. Moving the hole away from the damage was normally the quickest solution, then overseeding the area to promote new grass growth. Sometimes the idiots would just snap the flag poles. The poles took some work to break, as they were extremely flexible, but when they did snap the fiberglass shards would explode, leaving shrapnel all over the green. Sometimes just the flag itself would be removed from the pole and taken as a souvenir. Then there were the golfers that thought they were better players than they actually were. They would miss an easy putt, have a meltdown and smash their putters into the green, leaving dents in the ground.

But it seemed the most alluring targets to vandalize were the tunnel walls. There subterranean location made them a perfect target to vandalize and not be disturbed. Out of sight from the roads, the vandals could work on their "art" and not be seen.

Too bad they had no artistic skills and just made a mess on the concrete walls.

As I made my way around the course to collect the empty cans from the weekend. I noticed some new artwork was added to the tunnel that transitioned between the 3rd and 4th holes. The bright paint was uninspired in its design, with just the regular zig zags of color splashed on the concrete wall. I made a plan that later in the day I would return to paint over the mess, giving the vandals a clean wall to paint next weekend. On the way back to the shop I approached the tunnel from the other direction. There was a gold shimmer radiating out of the tunnel, a sparkling gold shape formed as I got closer. I laughed as I exited the tunnel. I parked my cart outside the tunnel and walked back into the coolness of the shaded concrete. From the approach back into the tunnel the shape was gone, I walked deeper into the tunnel to get a look from the other way. It appeared again, fascinating, this paint was only visible from the single direction. I laughed again, there it was in front of me, a five-foot-long golden penis. It was crude in form, head, shaft, balls. But there was no denying the artists intent. It was a giant golden dick. I chuckled as I went back to my cart, returning to the shop to get some paint.

Drew was in the shop getting a quick snack. I asked if he had seen the new artistic addition to the tunnel. He had not been that way yet today, so he had not. I asked if he wanted to help paint the tunnel, he did. We gathered the rollers, a few brushes and a can of grey paint and returned to the cool darkness of the tunnel. We took our time and painted over the colorful art with the grey paint. The grey absorbed into the concrete and disappeared as it dried, taking the graffiti with it. We finished painting over the spray-painted areas, all that was left was the golden dick. We paced the length of the tunnel, our focus on the wall. You really could only see it from the one direction. So, we decided to leave it alone, at least for awhile. We were curious to see if anyone would complain. Drew pulled out his brush and started to giggle. The brush reaching deep into the almost empty can of grey paint. He started to paint above the gold, chuckling to himself as he moved along the shaft. Once finished he took a step back to admire his handy work. we both were laughing as we left the tunnel, knowing, soon we would be called back to finish the job.

Tuesday is ladies' day. The women played each week in the league, competing for prizes and bragging rights. This would surely be the day that a complaint about the golden tunnel art would be placed. It was already noon and so far, nothing. Most of the ladies had finished their rounds and were back at the clubhouse having lunch. Drew and I finished our lunch, then went out to the tunnel. The final group of women were walking down the path, just entering the tunnel.

"I told you it was good luck!" the one lady chirped as the were halfway through the tunnel. Her voice with a slight echo. "I got par on the last three holes, and a birdie on the one before that." She explained with excitement. As the group exited the tunnel the lady with the newfound luck looked towards us. "I hope you guys aren't here to paint the tunnel." She said disappointedly.

"No, why?" I asked, holding in my laughter.

"There's a golden dick in tunnel and I rubbed it for good luck." She said managing to keep a straight face. "I think I'm going to win some prizes this week."

Drew and I looked at each other and burst out laughing. There was nothing funnier than an old lady talking trash. The group of golfers giggled as the walked off to the final tee box. The lucky lady continuing about her chances to win this week's treasures.

A few more days went by, and nothing was said about the half-completed job we did on the tunnel walls. On occasion you would see a female player walking down the tunnel, dragging their fingers across the golden paint. I found this hilarious. The legend of the golden penis and the luck that it provided was growing. Then finally one morning Lee was making his rounds and traveled back through the tunnel, with the light angled just right, so he could see the unmistakable shape of the golden penis.

Drew and I got called into Lee's office after lunch. We were barely seated when Lee started with

"What's with the golden dick in the tunnel?" Lee interrogated. The first step to any good interrogation is denial. Never admit to anything. Ever.

"What tunnel?" I asked, choking back a giggle. Lee was easy to wind up and when you got him going, comedy gold just waiting to happen. Every time.

"The one with the big dick painted on the side!" he grilled.

"I don't know of any dicks in tunnels." I spoke again. Looking over at drew as he barely held in the laughs. "Can you describe this dick?" I asked, a smile forming on my face.

"The one in the god damn tunnel with "suck me beautiful" painted in grey over the balls." He barked, steam starting to come out his ears. We broke and started to laugh.

"Oh, that tunnel dick." I said with an insincere surprise.

"Yes, that one." Lee said, "why has it not been painted over?" he asked.

"We can't paint over it, it's lucky, ask anyone." I said excitedly. Drew was still barely holding it together. As Lee was about to blow a gasket, his wife popped her head into the office to see what all the commotion was about. She had just finished her game and was returning the private cart she used every week.

Lee looked over to her and asked, "Did you notice anything strange in the tunnel today?"

She took a moment and thought about it, and answered "No, nothing out of the ordinary, just the lucky golden dick." She turned and left before Lee's face turned red.

"See, I told you it was lucky." I said in a cheeky tone.

"Go, get out of here!" Lee barked, pointing at the door. As we walked out, I could hear him muttering "stupid golden dicks." The golden paint stayed on the wall for the remainder of the season. Its hilarious legend grew as every week the players would run their fingers down the wall hoping for better luck. You never mess with people's luck.

Chapter 19: Camping Out on Four

I was driving the greens mower out of the lucky tunnel making the approach to the fourth green. I had gotten out a few minutes early to cut the greens and was ahead of schedule. Saturday mornings were great. All I needed to accomplish for the day was to cut all the greens, then I could go home. If I started early, I could be home sooner. The rumble of the mower echoed up the hill towards the green. As my eyes adjusted to the morning light, I could see something on the green. As the mower bounced down the cart path, my eyes started to clear and focus. The mower moved along at a steady speed, as the path bent along the edge of the channel. As I made the corner I could see, a plaid sleeping bag, laid out on the green. As I got closer and the mower rumbled along, the occupants of the sleeping bag awoke. I was about halfway up the hill as they sprung from their slumber. The male grabbed the sleeping bag and ran towards the fence. The lady grabbed up a pile of clothes and followed. What a way to start the day, having people run down the fence line in their underwear. They passed out of view as I got to the green. I got off the mower and walked up to the flag, pulling it from the cup. I gave the area a quick survey and saw nothing out of place. They must have decided to camp out overnight on the green. No damage was done, so I went on about my business. Monday morning, I told all the boys of the weekend encounter with the crazy kids in their underwear running down the course. Kelly chuckled as he recalled his encounter the weekend before. Must have been the same people out there, I couldn't imagine two sets of people sleeping out on the golf course. Kelly asked if they left anything behind. I told him no, nothing. He told me I was lucky, as the week before there were used rubbers scattered on the green. He told me he used the cart signs to pick them up and dispose of them in the grass trailer. I laughed at his misfortune and confirmed that I definitely did not have the same experience. For the following few weekends we kept an eye out for the sexy campers, but they never returned. Well, if they did come back, they were gone by the time we exited the tunnel. We never saw them or any evidence of their overnight shenanigans again.

As we shared our story of half naked people on the course Kelly made mention of the siren of 18. I have never seen it personally but as the legend goes, if you happen to be out on the 18th green early in the morning you might be fortunate enough to catch a glimpse of the siren of 18. Up in the high window of one of the houses that bordered the eighteenth fairway lived a middle-aged woman. As she started the day, she would stand topless in front of her window, showing the world her store-bought boobies. I was told that the work was well done, but never got to make the confirmation for myself.

Chapter 20: Cook Kelly

Kelly was the cook at the course kitchen. His girlfriend worked as a waitress in the restaurant. He had been there for a couple of years and was good at making the uninspired food. The menu was basic with only a handful of classic choices. The players were not expecting a fancy culinary experience so the burgers that were served were met with full acceptance. The stories that played out in the kitchen were ridiculous.

One evening Kelly was telling a story of some sexual nature in his animated fashion. While in the middle of his story he grabbed Chad, one of the other chiefs by the hips and gyrated behind him, exaggerating the story further. The other chef was not impressed by the simulated sex act and immediately put an end to it. The others laughed and continued to listen to the conclusion of Kelly's dirty story. The scorned chef seethed in the humiliation, vowing to take vengeance on Kelly's vulgar display. Chad rushed out of the kitchen and went straight into Lanny's office to lodge his complaint.

Lanny returned a short time later to the kitchen to collect more information on what had happened, so that he would be able to make a more informed decision on how to proceed.

Asking some questions about the incident didn't yield any results. The other chefs were not huge fans of Chad and didn't want to see Kelly get punished for his humorous story. Kelly tried to make a half-hearted apology, and it was met with unacceptance. Lanny was satisfied with the apology, but Chad was pissed at the results and threatened to get a lawyer involved. Lanny fearing litigation said that he would sort it out before it would need to be escalated to a court room. With Chad's threat of legal action, the kitchen environment instantly went toxic. Lanny went back to his office to work on an agreeable solution. The following day Kelly was called to the office and was told of his fate in the kitchen. Kelly was to be exiled to course maintenance. This would put distance between him and Chad and give time for the incident to blow over, before it went into a lawyer's office. Kelly agreed to the change in vocation. Chad was informed later in the day that Kelly was out of the kitchen and that seemed to calm the situation.

Kelly was in his mid twenties and was a good addition to the maintenance crew. His stocky frame made him good at moving heavy things and making it look easy. He must have had some golf course experience on his resume as he was given the prestigious honor of being the greens mower pilot. He was good at keeping the greens mowed to perfection. The stripes were always straight and crisp.

Chad was back in the kitchen trying to do his best, but the well had been poisoned and the others were not impressed that Kelly was gone. Chad's whiney attitude made him an easy mark to be picked on and teased. Kelly was the life of the party in the kitchen and with him gone the environment turned into a negative void. Chad did his best to keep up with his duties, but the others were giving him the cold shoulder and sabotaging his efforts at every possible opportunity. The idea of teamwork in the kitchen had died. Chad worked there for a few more weeks to see if the environment would recover, it never did, so he quit. Chad was angry about his departure and worked in the shadows to get his justice.

Kelly was in the shop one morning looking defeated. His normal high energy personality was deflated. I walked over to see what the problem was.

"Hey man, what's up?" I asked. "You look like your dog died."

Kelly looked up with fear in his eyes "I got served." He said.

"I always knew you were a dancer, why didn't you just bust a move" I made jest in reference to the title of a just released dance off movie. Kelly was a fat guy and the thought of him being a break dancer was funny too me.

He smiled back at me "Not that kind of served, asshole, and really?" he said as he jiggled his belly "I'm no dancer." "I got lawyer papers today over the kitchen incident." "I need to go to court over that bullshit." He said.

"Well, that can't be good" I said. Not knowing anything about the legal process on such a trivial incident. "When do you need to be there?" I asked.

"In a week" he said nervously.

"I'm sure you will get the death penalty." I told him. He smiled at the joke, knowing that the punishment certainly wouldn't be that.

The week went by fast, and Kelly needed to take an afternoon off to face his day in court. He arrived wearing a nice shirt and tie. Waiting with fearful anticipation for the proceedings. Chad was there too, also dressed in an ironed shirt and tie. They met each other's gaze from across the room. Both stared back at each other with contempt. They stood behind their respective tables next to the hired lawyers. The judge walked out and the room of people up out of respect. The judge gave a little wave as he sat in his chair.

"Please be seated." He spoke. The people sat. The judge cleared his throat and began to speak. "let's make this quick, will the plaintiff and the defendant please stand up." Chad and Kelly rose to their feet, each taking a moment to readjust their ties. The judge's focus locking onto Chad. "You are going to have a tough time if every little thing is going to cause you offence in the work force unless you grow some tougher skin." He paused, "don't be such a baby." "And you." The judge turning to Kelly with a finger pointed. "Keep your hands to yourself, this behavior is unacceptable." The judge said sternly. "The court does not have time for this type of childish dispute, dismissed." The judge stood up and left his bench. Chad and Kelly were ushered from behind the desk out of the courtroom.

Kelly let out a huge sigh of relief, as his expectations of punishment melting off his shoulders. Chad walked out with a pout, expecting to be handed a moral victory for his embarrassment. Both left the building without making any contact with each other. The case was closed.

Kelly returned to the shop the following day with news of his victory. He explained how he a been terrified of the potential outcome, expecting to be hauled off to jail for his transgression. He was happy on how it played out, and publicly stated that the whole experience was going to permanently change his behavior. It was good to see that he had learned a lesson from his shenanigans. I took note of the lesson and learned from his mistake. You can always learn from others; their missteps can teach a lot. Keep your hands to yourself. It seems simple enough that a rule we were taught as children would play such a large role as adults. Kelly stayed with us for the remainer of the season but decided to move on in the fall.

Chapter 21: Rude

My parents had just returned home from their scheduled Saturday round of golf. Dad bust in the door, bringing his clubs into the workshop. He would clean them later in the week, so that they would be perfect for next weekends round. The bag had barely found its balance on the floor and dad was rushing back outside. He was on a mission. I followed him out, curious to see what all the hustle was for. He seemed agitated and angry, and I wanted to find out why. Mom was still pulling her shoes out of the trunk when he went past. Mom looked up as dad started to cross the street.

"Be nice" she shouted as he went across the road.

"What's that all about?" I asked.

"Oh, dad's just going to go fight some kids from over on fifteen." She said with very little concern.

"Why would he want to do that." I asked.

Mom went on to tell me "The kids were talking trash." "We were putting on hole fifteen, and the kids started to taunt us from their yard," mom explained. "When they saw that your father had missed his putt, they went crazy." "Hooting and hollering, teasing your dad on his golf style." "Your dad marched over to the wall and barked back." "Then they told him with a what are you gonna do about it." "You know dad, he's not one to take any shit, so he told them that he would be by later to straighten them out." Being that he was a man of his word, that's where he was going. Mom retold the encounter and chuckled. Not expecting anything drastic to come of it. The neighborhood could always use a little bit more drama anyway.

I stood on the driveway and patiently waited for his return, eager to hear how it played out.

The fifteenth green was the closest hole of the course to our house. It was at the bottom of the hill. The green was set between the channel and the houses that backed onto the course. There were large trees that sheltered the houses from the onslaught of golf balls. The house in question had a large back yard. The yard was leveled out from its back door with a large retaining wall built to keep the ground flat. This provided the kids with an elevated advantage when trash talking the players. The shoulder high retaining wall was constructed from red bricks and looked like a fortress from the green. The trees had grown tall over the wall and provided a dark shade along the edge of the course.

Dad returned a short while later, with a smug grin on his face. Mom and I were standing on the driveway.

"What happened over there?" I asked, waiting impatiently for his story.

He took a deep breath and told us his story. "I went over and knocked on the door, the mother answered." "I asked if the boys lived there and described them." "Then I asked if I could speak to the little bastards." "She was not impressed and told me that he was being rude." "She was sure her little angles would never behave in that way." "Just as she said that I could see the little shits lurking in the house. So, I barked in at them." Dad then grinned as he recounted making his empty threats of bodily harm, by quoting his favorite wrestlers. "I told them I was gonna "polish up my clubs until they shined real nice, turn them sideways, then stick it up their candy ass." "The mom was not impressed and told me I was being rude." "I told her that if they pulled any of that nonsense next week I would come back." Dad was grinning as he finished the story. "I left the mother speechless; she was only able to tell me that I was rude." "Then closed the door." "I'm sure she hurried off to warn the children about my crazy warnings." Dad was self aware of his antics and had a look of satisfaction on his face. Thinking he had solved the problem. For the rest of the week any time dad said something cheeky we would mock him with a "don't be rude." In a pitchy voice. This made him crazy and making us laugh.

The following Saturday my dad thought that the message delivered from the week before would have solved his problems on hole 15. Well, he was wrong. The boys were waiting for him. Playing in the yard, watching for him to approach the green. The noise started the moment my dad walked onto the fringe of the green. They boys from their elevated yard hurled insults and mocked his game. Trying to lure him into the shade of the trees that grew tall below the retaining wall. As he approached the wall, the blast of hose water rained down. The water falling on the dense leaves of the trees, failing to hit their intended target. My dad rushed back onto the green with only a few droplets of water on his golf shirt. Shaking his fist and vowing retribution. My dad continued with his game. It was going to take more than some hose water to get under my dad's skin. Ignoring the taunts from above my parents finished the hole quickly, before the kids could reposition the hose to have better aim. Hoping to calm the situation, Mom talked Dad out of going back to their house after the game. By time they got back home all his anger had subsided and he had forgotten about the boys' lame attempt with the hose.

The next week my father was on maximum awareness on hole 15. Waiting for the kids to pull another round of tricks. As he approached the green, the hole was quiet, too quiet. In the silence he could he a muffled chatter coming from up in the yard. A giggle escaped, and a quick "shush" put back the silence. The leaves of the trees blocked the view into the yard, but Dad knew the kids were there, plotting. He was not going to be lured into the range of the hose this week. He planned to stay out of the trees altogether. Walking over to his ball, that rested only ten feet from the hole. He Lined up his putt and took the shot. My mother walked quickly over to the flag and pulled it from the cup. The ball dropped into the hole. Dropping the flag off on the edge of the green, my mother made her shot, tapping in her final stroke. She walked back to the edge of the green to gather the flag. My dad reached into the hole to grab the balls. Mom's ball was retrieved without a problem. Dad pulled his ball from the hole found it stuck to the bottom of the cup. He removed the ball and found it covered in a thick, brown, sticky substance. As he stood up, the kids in the yard bust into laughter. They had put maple syrup into the cup, making the first ball into the hole to come out covered in the brown sugary slime. My parents did not see them on the green before they tee off, so other groups must have also been victims to this prank. My dad barked empty insults and threats into the yard. And the kids just laughed harder. Mom and Dad walked off the green to continue the round. Dad was mad and plotting revenge. Mom shot down the idea, raising her finger and saying, "Don't be rude." Her laugh echoed as they walked past the porta-loo into the corrugated tunnel. Dad seethed for the rest of the round. Plotting his vengeance.

We had just finished dinner when dad gave me the nod across the table. It was a cheeky little nod that let me know he was planning some sort of trickery.

"Thomas and I have to run to the office." "Don't you want those copies made for your homework?" He was laying it on thick. I didn't have any homework. I didn't even know what he was talking about, but I agreed anyway.

"Sure, lets go." I said. We left the table and went down to the basement. "So, where are we really going?" I asked.

"I need a lookout." He said. Dads' medication had probably kicked in, so I had no idea what he had planned.

"Sure, ok whatever you need." I said sarcastically.

He noticed my lack of commitment to the mission and gave me more details. "I'm gonna fix those kids on fifteen, they won't know what hit 'em." He said with a maniacal grin. The look of mischief in his eyes sparked my interest.

"Sounds good, let's go." I said.

We put our shoes on, leaving through the garage. We crossed the street. No cars were anywhere in sight. We normally eat early, around five. It was just after six, and the other houses were just starting dinner. We walked through the gap in the divided fence. We were almost at the yard in question. We stopped one house away and listened. We waited a few moments before Dad opened up about his plans.

"Those little shits keep trying to get me with the hose, this will teach them." Dad said with a chuckle.

We could hear voices coming from their back yard. The kids were back there playing. His plan was to use the hose on the side of their house to blast them with their own water. We crept up to the hose reel and quietly unraveled the hose. The rings of the hose laid out nicely, with the hose ready to be pulled quickly, without getting tangled. Dad had the nozzle at the ready. The hose was equipped with a multidirectional nozzle. He clicked the selector to make his choice to the jet. I turned the tap and watched as the hose expanded as it filled with water. We walked to the side gate quietly, not wanting to give away or positions. With dad at the ready, I pulled the string that hung through the fence and opened the latch. The gate wasn't even fully open before Dad bust through. Squeezing the water nozzle tight, he took aim at the closest child. I was right behind dad not wanting to miss out on any of the hilarity. The look of panic as they recognized my father standing in their yard was electric.

Dad sprayed the first kid while shouting "How do you like the hose now boys!" he taunted. The second kid was just figuring out what was going on as the hose was turned in his direction. Before they even had time to shout about the intrusion to their parents, the boys were dripping wet. Completely soaked. I was laughing hard, as the boys looked like drowned rats.

"This better be the end of you fuckin around on Saturdays." Dad warned "Or I'll be back."

I was only paying attention to the kids in the yard, not noticing that their father was standing on the deck. He was behind the barbeque flipping burgers. The look of confusion on his face was priceless. Their dad started to raise objection, just as my dad turned the hose towards the hot grill. The sizzle of the water as it hit the back of the barbeque caused the other Dad to jump back. He was still unable to process what had just happened.

"Control your damn kids." Dad said as he dropped the hose. We left the yard and returned home with haste. Once we were back in the garage we started to laugh. My sides hurt from the laughing so hard. We made enough noise for mom to come down and see what was going on. She knew right away we were up to no good.

"What did you do?" she asked sternly. Knowing that this type of laughter on comes after something ridiculous.

I could barely get the words out as I retold the tale. "Dad and I went over to the house on 15 and blasted the kids with the hose." I said between laughs. "I think dad even got their dad while he was cooking." I finished with another heavy laugh.

Dad was still giggling when mom asked, "What if they call the police, what are you gonna tell them?"

Dad stopped for a second, looking up as if in deep thought, "Fuck 'em", then burst out laughing again. Mom shook her head and went back into the house.

The cops never showed up. Dad never got sprayed with the hose on the fifteenth hole ever again, the boys never taunted over the wall. I don't know what happened at the house on fifteen, but I'm sure the kids had some explaining to do. That must have been a funny conversation explaining why an adult was in the yard with the hose. Dad was definitely being rude, but hey they started it.

Chapter 22: Masters of the Water Box

One spring morning I was told by Lee that today would be the day that I would learn how the course irrigation system works. After every winter, as the frost comes out of the ground, a few of the underground pipes would need to be replaced. The course had miles of underground irrigation pipes. I was instructed into the back supply room to go get some of the supplies needed to go fix a pipe break that had just occurred. I went into the back room and grabbed a tin of blue primer and a tin of the grey pipe glue. I put them into the back of the golf cart, then went over to the spot on wall near the big door and collected a flat shovel and a spade. I was also told grab a plastic drinking cup, that we would be needing to bail out any of the extra water that lingered in the bottom of the soon to be dug out hole. Lee walked out of the supply room in the front of the building, holding some pipe pieces and the chain wrench. He also dropping them into the back box of the cart. We sat in the cart, and I was instructed to drive over to the fourth hole. As we got closer Lee modified the directions to the destination and we parked at the bottom of the fairway, just left of the tee boxes.

I parked the cart at an angle between the broken pipe location and the tee box to provide some cover when the players started to take their shots. We got out of the cart, and I grabbed the shovels. There were always telltale signs that something was broken underground. This pipe break had blasted a hole into the ground when the water burst out. Making half of the hole I needed to dig already done. I started to dig around the effected area. Stepping hard on the shovel to break the surface of the sod. Making a square and finally pulling the grass by the hair off the ground. Tossing the freshly scalped piece to the side, where it would sit until its replacement after the pipe was fixed. Digging into the wet ground was easy, the soft dirt being pulled from the earth without much effort. The shovel had moved all the ground that it could, so I knelt and used my hands to remove the rest to clear out the area thoroughly. When I had completed pulling enough mud from the hole, I looked at Lee and asked if that was good enough. He nodded his approval and sat down next to the hole.

My first instruction was to use the saw to cut the pipe where it was broken. Back and forth the saw went cutting through the pipe with ease. Moving to the other side of the pipe and repeating the cut proved to be slightly more difficult, the pipe was no longer ridged, it bounced with each stroke from the saw. I Appling some downward pressure to the pipe, giving it some stability and making the job quicker. When the saw was finished the pipe broke free with a satisfying snap. Pulling out the broken piece of pipe and giving it an inspection, the top was in perfect condition, the bottom of the pipe however was fractured into a spiral of sharp plastic teeth. None of the pipe was missing but the water pressure managed to explode out the bottom of the pipe.

I was then told to go to the cart and grab the parts Lee had brought out of the storeroom. I grabbed the compression coupling; it would be the solution for this break. The compression coupling was a pipe with threaded twist caps on each end. I was instructed to unscrew each cap. There were holes in the caps that fit over the broken pipe and inside the caps were rubber seals. I disassembled the coupling and put a cap on each end of the break. The caps slid over the uncovered pipe with ease. I reached in with the center portion of the coupling and adjusted it into place. Tightening the one end cap then sliding the other cap down the broken pipe until it met the threads of the center coupling. The coupling was longer than the piece I had cut out. It rested on each side of the gap with the broken pipe being inside. Reaching into the hole and using my hands I tightened the caps as best I could, then using the chain wrench I twisted the caps until they were snug. I was told not to make the caps too tight, or they would crack. The chain wrench was a perfect tool for the job. The flexibility of the chain lets you get leverage around the caps with a minimal amount of working space. Lee looked over the work, approved of its completion and instructed for the hole to be filled. I replaced the dirt and put the chuck of lawn back over the freshly overturned ground.

Over the next few weeks Drew and I got to be Lee's water box apprentices. We learned the tricks and skills to fix any pipe break. The replacement of rain bird sprinkler heads became a large part of the program. Sometimes the heads wouldn't pop, and the problem would need to be traced back to the electrical components of the system.

We were called out to the twelfth green where the sprinkler heads were not working. The rainbirds would not pop up and we didn't find any of the signs of a pipe break. Lee thought it might be the solenoids. We found the electrical box off to the left of the cart path. Popping off the green plastic cover with the hook tool, the cover made a satisfying vacuum sound as it pulled away from its overgrown resting place. The box in ground box made a nice sized cavern into the earth, it was easy to work in, but we needing to replace the power supply, we would require more space than was available, so we started digging.

After the hole was large enough to get our hands around the module we called Lee over. He got down on his knees and leaned into the freshly opened ground. Holding a flashlight in one hand and a screwdriver in the other he began to tinker with the module.

Looking up from the hole at us Lee said, "You should always turn the power off when you do this type of job." Continuing to prod the module, a spark flashed in the hole. Lee's body gave a jolt, a mumble of profanity escaped his lips. The screwdriver returning to the hole, another spark. After a surprisingly blue blast of profanity, Lee stood up from the hole and began to walk over to the power box that was only a few feet away. Opening the front panel and pulling down the power breaker, with a large clack, into the off position. "I probably should have done that sooner." He joked.

Drew and I looked at each other and chuckled. Lee was a character and him being electrocuted was funny. After a few moments of tinkering back in the hole on the module, Lee proclaimed victory. I was instructed to go to the water valve and give it a small twist. I turned the knob slowly and the rainbird heads started to sputter and spit. The sprinkles began to shoot water toward the green. A few feet from the valve the ground began to swell, looking like a balloon under the grass. Moments later the ground erupted, water shooting into the air. I quickly spun the valve back into the off position. The water pressure blasted a good deal of the ground out of the way, but now we would have to dig down to find the broken pipe to make the required repair.

I grabbed the flat head shovel and began to dig the hole. The ground was soft and moved out easily. I had a two-foot-deep hole dug and could still not see the broken pipe. I continued to dig, the hole got deeper and deeper. Once the hole was as deep as my shovel was tall you could see the break. Lee walked over and investigated the hole. The pipe had a large chunk missing from the top. I had abandoned the regular shovel and was now laying on the ground with a small hand shovel cleaning out the remainder of the mud around the pipe. It was still early in the day and the ground was still cold. Lee grabbed the saw and instructed me out of the hole. He laid down on the soggy grass and reached deep into the hole. He began to cut the pipe; his movement was difficult with the odd angle of approach and minimal leverage. It did not help any that the hole was beginning to fill up with water. The ground was saturated at that depth and water always finds the path of least resistance. The fresh hole was a perfect location for the water to settle into. Looking for a better position Lee looked out from the hole at Drew and I

"Hold my legs boys, I'm going in." Lee's voice echoed as he submerged his head into the ground.

The hole swallowed him until he was almost in up to his belt. His hand would sporadically emerge, fingers wiggling for a part or tool that we would instinctively know and send it back. Sometimes we would hand him the same tool twice just to see the frustration grow. A blast of unintelligible mumbles would exit the hole. On this occasion the hole was quite large and there were a few inches of water below the broken pipe. So, as we were holding Lee's legs, we gave him a quick little dip. His hair got submerged in the muddy water at the bottom of the hole. His arms reached back, and he extracted himself from the hole looking like a drowned rat. His hair was covering his forehead and mud was running down his cheeks. He shot us a look of WTF, wiped the mud from his face and went straight back into the hole to tighten the coupling. Drew and I looked at each other, a flash of trickery sparked in our eyes. We dipped Lee into the hole again. His legs kicking, we pulled him back out. Twisting his head back, hair dripping from the dirty water.

"Hold my legs, I've almost got it." And he dove back into the hole. Before we could get a grip on his coveralls, his legs were kicking. We pulled him back out of the hole, he had been up to his eyes in the muck. There was mud over his brow and his hair was soaked. Lee sat up and collected his breath. Drew looked at each other and busted out laughing.

"You look like a drowned rat!" I joked. Lee's hand reaching up to realign his hair, as muddy water dripped down his face.

"You guys can finish this one." he said. "I'm going to get cleaned up." Lee turned and went to his cart.

Grabbing the bailer buckets from the work cart we began to empty the hole. The bailing worked well; we were able to get water out of the hole faster than it returned. We wasted no time in cutting the second half of the pipe and making the repair. The compression coupling going into position without any hassle. With the pipe fixed we put up some rebar and rope around the hole, to make a safety fence to keep people from falling in. We then returned to the shop for some lunch. Planning on filling the hole in the afternoon.

Once we returned to the hole, the ground had started to dry out around the edge. Placing the protective plastic box over the module, was started using the shovels to fill the hole. We dumped the dirt back into the space around the box. Once the ground was level with the open box, the grass was replaced around the perimeter of the plastic and the cover was stepped back into place. The sprinklers around the green were ready to be tested again.

I looked over at the twelfth green, and a group of ladies were just finishing their final strokes. I walked over to the sprinkler box and waited for them to finish. After the flag was replaced, and they were all walking off to the next hole, I was ready to start the test. I dropped my hand into the sprinkler box, my fingertips touching the small valve. I twisted the knob and looked back towards the green. One of the ladies had gone back for a forgotten club on the fringe. The sprinkler heads spat out a burst of air, then rested back into the ground. She stopped, confused by the sound that had just gasped between her legs. After a momentary hesitation the sprinkler blasted out of the ground. She let out a scream. The main direction of water going behind her, the tail of the sprinkler shooting out in front. I reached back into the hole, fumbling to get the valve. I managed to spin the valve off before the sprinkler head started its path of rotation. There was a fresh mist in the air in front of the startled golfer. Her position over the sprinkler was ideal. If the sprinkler raised in any other direction, she would have been hit with a direct shot and would have most likely been soaked. She rushed back over to her friends too explained the shriek that she had let out. I could hear them laughing in the distance. Now that the green was clear again, I turned the sprinklers on full blast. They worked as expected. Without any more visible leaks, I was satisfied with the job.

By the end of the season, I knew where every module, sprinkler, or main valve shut off was located. There were a few abandoned boxes throughout the course that were empty, except for the bugs that took up residence. The sprinklers were designed to cover the greens, tee boxes and fairways with an even distribution of water. The water supplied to the course was provided by the river. Inside the pump house was a deep well, it was protected by the walls of a shack. The small unassuming house structure was setoff of the course, closer to the river. Its giant pump would push water to all corners of the grounds as required. The equipment inside let out an electric buzz that was barely audible unless you were next to the building. The well would be filled with the water from the river and was in abundant supply. However, an hour worth of rain would keep the grass greener than a week's worth of sprinkler water. We would try and run the sprinklers manually in the afternoons to keep the overhead sun from scorching the greens. The sprinklers were setup to run off timers at night. Turning the sprinklers on in the afternoon was the best task on a hot summer day. I would park the cart just outside of the sprinkler radius, walking over to the valve, turning on the water. Then I would return to the cart and wait for the golfers to approach the green. This was my signal to turn off the water. While I waited, I would enjoy the local rock station on my radio and close my eyes. Every minute you could sit in the sun with your eyes shut was pure heaven. The mist from the sprinklers floating over, providing a nice cooldown from the summer heat. On more than one occasion, I fell into a slumber waiting for the next group of golfers to arrive. With the clearing of a throat, I would be awakened, immediately springing into action to shut off the water. I would then race to the next green, turning the water on, and try to find another cat nap.

Chapter 23: War With the Marshals

I cut the holes for a couple of months; people knew it was me that placed them around the greens. Some of the players were not happy with me. I was the excuse that they would use, blaming me for the extra strokes on their game. When confronted with this, I would just tell them that they would need to keep practicing, and that they are not as good as they thought they were. I was ruthless. However, my infamy became so prevalent that I could no longer eat dinners at the club house restaurant without being confronted with jeers from the players of how I cost them strokes each week.

One Friday I was in the hallway with my father waiting to be seated in the restaurant. Willing to take the chance of a confrontation for some delicious chicken fingers. We were approached by one of the marshals. Brian was an old British fellow. He would work on the course trying to keep the players from taking to long on each hole. He was always friendly and would greet me with a wave and a smile when we crossed paths. Brian walked up and started to talk about the flag placement of hole thirteen. I just grinned. Knowing that he was not going to get me to concede the placement of the holes for not meeting his satisfaction. He started to converse with my dad.

"Hey Glen, did Thomas tell you how good my new swing is?" he asked. "I, was showing him earlier this week." Brian said, looking over to me for approval for his swing.

"It looked kind of fruity ass to me." I proclaimed.

Anger crept into Brian's eyes, and with a flash, he tried to kick me in the nuts. I took a quick step back, just to be missed. His fleeting attempt to cause equivalent pain that I caused damaging his ego made my dad let out a chuckle. Brian turned in a huff and left us standing there. We started laughing with each other.

My dad looked at me and asked, "Did he just try to kick you in the nuts?"

"Yes" I responded. We laughed even harder, as we waited for our table. The swing in question was one where on the follow through, your arms would loop back around your head with a strange shoulder roll. Definitely fruity ass.

The following week after the encounter with Brian in the restaurant lobby, I told the boys of how Brian tried to kick me in the nuts for saying his golf swing was fruity ass. They all laughed at the near miss of my family jewels. So I suggested we get some vengeance, and declared open season on the marshals.

That afternoon the sun was hot, as I was driving back to the shop to get some ice-cold water, I saw the marshal cart. It was unoccupied and parked next to the channel. The golf cart made almost no noise as I approached the unattended cart. I stopped next to the empty cart. Got out of mine and jumped into the marshal's ride, and drove it up the fairway, parking it behind some trees. The cart would not be completely invisible but would take some time scouting to locate it. I then ran back to my cart and continued on the journey to get a cold refreshment.

After getting my drink, I returned past the scene of the crime. Marshal Brian was walking up the hill back towards where his cart had been. His hands were full of the golf balls he found searching in the tall grass. He reached the top of the hill at the exact spot where his cart should have been. A look of confusion crossed his face.

I stopped and asked, "how is you day going, Brian?" Grinning ear to ear. I had guilty written all over my face. Brian's confusion quickly turned to anger as the old Englishman instantly knowing I had something to do with the misplaced vehicle.

"Where is it?" he forcefully asked.

"What?" I asked choking back a giggle.

"My cart, where did you take it?" he demanded.

I feigned ignorance and took off. "Good luck!" I shouted over my shoulder as I left.

Looking back, I could see some players approaching the marshal and pointing towards the treeline where the cart was poorly hidden. They must have been able to see it from the tee box. Brian was not amused, standing there with his balls in his hands. Upon retrieving his cart, the first stop he made was back to the shop to complain to Lee. He Complained about the theft of his cart and how he would not stand for it. And demanding that we be punished for such disrespect.

At the morning meeting the next day Lee made a friendly reminder not to take the carts from the Marshals or they would probably have a heart attack, and he would not be responsible for hiding the bodies. We all agreed that the marshal carts would not be moved and started in on the day. As the sun reached its peak and my water bottle was empty, I drove over to one of the water coolers. Noticing that the marshal was also at the cooler, as I made my approach. I got out of the cart and started to fill up my bottle. Marshal Brian walked over. He had a grin on his face, as if his tattletale put the fear into me.

"Don't mess with me, or my cart or I will have you fired." He stated.

I shrugged it off, giving back a "Yea, whatever." And continued to fill the bottle. Brian walked past me to speak to the golfers that were approaching the tee box. I tightened the lid to my bottle and got back in my cart. I drove the cart a few feet and stopped next to Brian's cart. I looked back, checking to see if the marshal's attention was still fully with the players, it was. I slid over the carts bench seat and leaned into his cart, removing the key and driving off. I was not too far when I heard the shout from behind. Not looking back, I raised my hand and gave a friendly wave as I drove out of sight.

For the next few weeks, I would leave the marshal alone. Brian would never leave his cart out of his line of sight anyway, and he started to carry a second key. Pulling the same tricks week after week was no fun. You had to keep them guessing if you wanted to reach the rank of master prankster. Building the tension of what possible shenanigans were coming next kept the hot summer afternoons interesting. After awhile Brian became complacent and would leave his cart unattended again, returning to his old habits of looking for golf balls in the tall grass.

Hiding in a cluster of trees, laying in the shade, with my belly on the ground, I waited. Stalking my prey. Watching as the cart wound up the path, closer to the position I required for some trickery. Turning the sprinklers on was not a guaranteed victory. It all was dependent on the direction that the sprinkler head stopped the last time it was used. On this occasion it worked out very well. I knew when the cart entered range of the rainbird sprinkler. My hand was deep in the sprinkler box, waiting for the perfect moment to twist the star shaped valve. I gave it a spin and the water blasted out of the sprinkler head. It was a direct hit. The water blasted the front side panel of the cart, spraying water up and onto the seat. Now Brian with his soggy pants was pissed. I was low on the ground and a hundred meters from the sprinkler that had just went off. This sprinkler box operated seven other heads, scattered around the fringe of the green. I jumped from behind the trees, waving over to Brian.

"Sorry, didn't see you there." I lied.

His head turning in my direction to get a good look at the culprit of his discomfort. I waved like an idiot, got into my cart and drove off. The sprinklers were left on for a while, until the next group of players would start the hole, then I quickly returned to shut the water off. Brian with his wet pants looking like he had an "accident" and went straight back to the shop to tell Lee.

Brian burst into the maintenance building to find Lee working at the shop bench on some newly started project.

"Look what Thomas did!" he stormed. Pointing to the wet pants "I'm pissed off."

Lee looking up from his task "You look pissed on" he said jokingly.

Brian said nothing, he was not amused and stormed off in a huff, knowing that no punishment would befall the perpetrator of his injustice. The battle lines had been drawn, and the teams were clearly defined. War was being declared and no one was going to escape the vengeful wrath of the marshals.

Retaliation started off slowly and unoriginal. Every time a marshal would pass one of the work carts they would stop and remove the keys. A slight inconvenience for sure, but we would not be tricked by our own tactics and always had extra keys close at hand. The marshals would pass by an unattended cart and spill out the contents of their water bottles onto the seat. Having the seat of your pants soaked was uncomfortable. We started to carry some extra towels used on the ball cleaning stations in the front of our carts. Becoming more cautious to double check the moisture of the seats before jumping blindly onto the cart.

One Saturday I was filling up the water coolers. I had the radio on and was lost in early morning thought. The marshal was making an early trip around the course setting up for a tournament that was taking place later in the day. He passed by the water station and waved as he went by. I thought nothing of it. My focus was lost in the music. I finished filling up the coolers and retuned to my cart, ready to proceed to the next station. I hit the accelerator and took off. On the next hole I found the marshal who was grinning wide. He stepped onto the cart path to slow me down. I removed my headset and stopped to see what he needed.

"Looks like you forgot something." He said with a big grin.

"I don't think so," I said, taking a quick inventory of the immediate area, not noticing anything missing.

"Ok then, have fun filling the next cooler." He said with a chuckle as he turned and walked back to his task.

I didn't move and took another look around to see what I was missing. Then I noticed how I had just been bamboozled. When the marshal had past me at the last water station he must have stopped outside my field of view. While my back was turned lost in the jams, the marshal pulled the pin from between the water cooler tank and my golf cart. When I drove away from the station the water cart dropped off from the hitch and was left behind. With my music loud I didn't here the thud of the water tank frame landing on the pavement.

I looked over to the marshal and waved. "Well played," I said loudly to cover the distance between us.

I then made the shameful U-turn to go retrieve the water tank. This was a good little trick and I played it a few time on the others over the years. Pulling trailer pins was always funny and inconvenient.

Once the boys were the collateral damage of my marshal feud, we devised new and more elaborate tactics to keep the marshals guessing of our tomfoolery. We started with the cart batteries. Removing one of the connections from the battery post would render the cart unmovable. The marshals making the initial inspection and seeing that the key was not the cause of the problem. Thinking the cart looked to be untampered with would need to be towed back to the club house. This worked for awhile, but the soon they became wise, as every trick has a lifespan.

As our creativity grew, so did the risks. The line might have been crossed when I pulled some proper sabotage on Brians cart. The cart was left next to the edge of the pond on the 12th hole. Brian was off in the rough looking for more lost golf balls to add to his collection. He had taken the key with him from the cart, so he felt that it would be safe as he wandered along the fence line. I walked over to the marshal's cart and lifted the seat. I made a quick disconnection and dropped the seat back into place. I reached down to the direction switch and moved it into the reverse position. The cart was facing out towards the fairway, its rear tires only two feet from the edge of the pond.

Brian returned a shot time later, placing the basket of found golf balls that he had gathered gently on the seat. He inserted the key and started the cart. Brian's foot pressed hard on the accelerator. The cart lunged backwards. Dropping the back tires off the muddy bank and into the pond. Brian was shocked and confused by the sudden reverse direction the cart had taken.

Normally when the cart was set to go backwards the backup warning tone would sound with its pulsing rhythm. But the cart had been silent, not giving him the backwards warning. He moved the direction lever to the forward position and tried to move. The tires of the cart spinning deeper into the mud, pulling the cart into the water. His cart had made it about halfway into of the pond, the back bumper submerged by the sinking cart. The cart had gotten high centered on the bank and was properly stuck. Brian had to step into the muck as he got out of the cart. The basket of balls had tipped over and spilled onto the floorboard. Some of balls had made it back into the water. Brian was furious. His shoes were soaked and covered in a heavy swamp mud. As he surveyed the area for the cause of his misfortune. We drove out from behind our tree covered vantage point, moving in the opposite direction from the "accident." The cart was stuck deep in the muck and slowly sinking, it would need some assistance to be pulled loose. Brian started on his heavy-footed walk back to the shop to find a tow. This would be the last straw. A truce was called a short time later. The final act of trickery was perpetrated on Lee. Once he was targeted, we knew that the fun was over, and we needed to take a rest on the pranks.

Lee was ready to make his morning rounds. He planned to check on the boys and make sure all was good. His old green and white ford F-100 was parked at the side entrance of the maintenance shop. This truck was his baby. It had been washed earlier in the morning and was spotless. As Lee approached the truck, he noticed a marshal cart on the other side of the shallow creek that divided the maintenance yard and the third hole. The marshal was out of the cart and poking in the creek water pulling out lost golf balls. The marshal had one eye on Lee and gave a wave as their eyes met. Lee waved back, reaching for the door handle of his truck. Lee, pressing hard on the door latch and opened the truck door. DING! A slight pause, then an onslaught of golf balls poured out the open truck door. Each one of the falling golf balls ringing off the running board of truck. The roar of balls avalanched out onto the pavement, bouncing and rolling into the creek. Marshal Brian was rolling on the ground with laughter. Lee was not impressed. Taking a step back to let all the balls escape the truck.

The marshals had been planning this attack for awhile. They all had managed to collect hundreds of garbage golf balls. Any balls with a slice or gouge out of their coating made the grade and were enlisted into the plan. They had managed to fill the truck from the floorboard to almost the top of the seat with damaged balls. The balls flowed out from the truck for five solid minutes, each one ringing off the running board, the sound became deafening as the onslaught continued. Golfers were looking on from the third tee box, concerned to see what this machine gun racket was. Lee waited for the last ball to hit the pavement, closed the truck door, and went back into the shop. He sat in his office and contemplated the terms of our surrender.

The boys and I returned to the shop around 930 for our scheduled snack break. Lee emerged from his office with a half smirk on his face.

"Well, boys." He started. "No more games with the marshals," he said. Then he told us about the truck and all the balls. "Today was the last straw, I didn't want go get involved, but maybe it has gone too far."

Collectively we laughed and admired the prank. Opening the side door of the shop to go admire the carnage. I was immediately surprised by the number of balls that now littered the pavement. It looked as if it snowed, but only in a concentrated area. The balls were mostly in a contained space, but some of the balls had bounced and managed to travel surprisingly far. Some had rolled into the grass down the hill and back into the creek. There was a large concentration of balls in the water, easy to find when the balls whiteness shimmers in the shallow water. We went back into the building and had our snacks. After break we went out and collected all the balls. There were well over five hundred balls scattered across the ground. The cease fire was called later that afternoon. There were no more ticks played that season.

Chapter 24: Waiting For the Fallout

The summer had been hot, and the world was in a strange place. 1999 was coming to an end. The Y2K fever was starting to take hold. The world was expecting to have all computers crash and become completely unusable. Planes were going to fall from the sky and the world would never be the same. All over some lazy computer code that didn't write the dates with years as four-digit numbers. The whole idea seemed crazy to me. I didn't spend much time entertaining the thought of the end of the world.

As I was working on the ninth tee box, spreading new grass seed into the divots left behind from the golfers. My hand digging deep into the burlap bag to grab the sharp seeds. My knuckles catching the tattered end of the bag as I pulled out a handful. Throwing the seeds in clumps to fill the deep scars on the tee top. As I reached into the bag for more seed, the sky got weird. It was a clear day, and the sky was a vibrant blue, the last time I noticed. I looked up, and off in the distance I could see it. I dropped the bag of seed on the ground and faced towards my expected doom. Waiting for the blinding flash and then the meat to be blasted off my bones. But nothing arrived. There it was in the distance, a mushroom cloud filled the blue sky with its ominous grey form, rolling into itself as it reached up into the sky. I watched it grow, waiting for shockwave to envelop everything just like the judgement day. The mushroom cloud from the initial explosion quickly morphed into a black funnel of smoke reaching high into the sky. Once I decided this was not the end of the world, I ran over to my golf cart and found my radio and tuned in for an update. The radio news was in a frenzy. The oil refinery in town had just exploded. The explosion sending the massive fireball into the sky, then raining down debris all over the nearby neighborhoods. Our course was far enough away to not be affected directly by the blast or any of the falling materials, but the smoke lingered in the air. It took hours to get the blaze under control. In the aftermath of the explosion two people had lost their lives. It was a tragic day for the city. August 9, 1999, a day that would be remembered for its explosive tragedy.

Chapter 25: Grabby Grandma

Drew and I were working on digging a trench along the main road towards the maintenance building. The players would walk down the road on their way to the final tee box. I had taken a moment to stand up straight and have a stretch. Looking down the road I could see Drew was only twenty feet away. He was hunched over pulling the top off a water box that was in our path. A group of old lady golfers were starting to walk past him. As the golfers passed by his location, one of the old birds reached down and grabbed Drew's butt. Drew stood up and looked back in my direction, with a look of shock on his face. The ladies continued their way.

He started to walk over to me. "I think that old lady just grabbed my ass!? He said. "I though it was you messing about, but then I looked up and you were over here." He said confused.

"Nope, wasn't me." I said starting to laugh. "Now your gonna end up with a grandma girlfriend." I joked.

"Ha, as if" drew said. "I need to go get an elbow segment; I'll be back." He said with a terminator accent. Drew got in the cart and drove towards the shop. As he passed the tee box, I could hear a cackle of laughter as the old ladies burst out in hysterics as the one told the others how she played some grab ass.

Chapter 26: On Call Sunday

I finished working hours ago. The pager on my belt beeped and vibrated with urgency. I was given a pager so that I could be reached if anything went wrong on the course after hours on the weekends. It's a golf course, what could go wrong? I looked down to see the shop number flash across the ten-digit display. I got my shoes on and went out to the car. I drove down to the shop, once the car crested the driveway onto the course maintenance road, I could see why I was called. There was a geyser of swamp water being blasted meters into the sky. I parked my car next the shop and went inside the building. I knew the tool for the job. I was looking for the long rebar t-handle water key. It was right where it was supposed to be. If you always put your tools away, you can always find them when they are critically needed. I walked out of the shop towards the blasting water. Lanny was standing off to the side, in the shadow of a pine tree. He was soaked and looking miserable. As I walked closer, he spoke up.

"I tried to turn it off" he said with defeat in his voice.

He was dressed in his fancy golf clothes and must have been playing when the pipe burst. Wanting to be the hero, he tried to turn off the water. I got closer, swinging the rebar as I walked. The water was muddy and dark. I reached into the funnel of water with the rebar, the bottom pegs finding the intended spot. Turning the key the water slowed. Once the water was less than waist height, I reached over and used both hands to twist the tools final rotations. The ground was soaking wet, and a huge hole was blasted out of the earth. Lanny looked over with fire in his eyes.

"How did you do that, so fast? He asked.

I replied with a snarky "When you call the best, you get the best."

I turned and walked back towards the shop to put back the water key. By this point I knew every sprinkler box and valve location on the course. I could find them in my sleep, with my eyes closed. I knew that this was a main valve, by the waterspout that shot up. So, feeling for a large hand valve to turn it off was the goal. I just happened to catch the edge on the first try with the key. There is no skill to turn a valve, but I did have some luck, making it look ridiculously easy. I got in the car and drove out the gate. Lanny was still standing by the open ground, dripping from his failed attempt, and still stunned by my quick success.

Monday after finishing the morning job of cutting the greens, I was instructed to go and repair the pipe that had burst over the weekend. It was the mainline. The four-inch diameter pipe that provided water to the front section of the course. The location of the break prevented the first three holes from being watered and needed to be repaired before the sun burnt the grass. This was going to be a bigger job, so I went to find some help. In the yard Megan was working at the green house, so I enlister her help. She was always interested in learning new skills and happy to help. Plus, any extra time, we got to spend together was just a bonus. We went into the shop and entered the back storage room. I flicked on the light switch and the bulb barely illuminated the room. Waiting for my eyes to adjust to the dim light, I reached to get some pipe glue. We collected the parts that I thought we would need, loaded them up and drove over to the crater on the third hole.

Looking into the hole, it was starting to cave in on the sides, water had filled the bottom making a giant mud pit. The blast from the broken pipe had made a giant hole in the ground so not too much digging was going to be required. I took off my shoes and put on some rubber boots. Megan did the same. I stepped into the hole. It was almost waist deep. I asked for the bucket so I could bail out the water at the bottom. Megan wanting to be helpful, also jumped into the hole, and we started to bail out the unwanted water. Once the pipe was visible, I moved some of the dirt from the edge of the hole, clearing enough room to use the hand saw. The pipe was thick, and I didn't have much elbow room. Cutting the pipe seemed to take an hour. Once the broken section was removed, I explained how we were going to make the repair. When I cut the pipe there was some space between the valve and the break. We would be able to add a coupling to extend the pipe away from the valve then use a compression coupling to fill in the gap. I removed the tight silver cap off the blue primer and instructed Megan to apply it to the pipe. The thin blue liquid adhering to the pipe with the soft applicator. I reached out with the pipe glue container, it's grey sticky mess eager to meet the primer. She applied the glue, and I reached over with the pipe coupling, slipping it onto the broken pipe. The excess glue seeping out from the gap between the two pieces.

"What now?" she asked.

I said "We have to wait for the glue to dry, but it would not take too long." I playfully ran my dirty fingers down her arm, leaving a trail of three muddy lines. She splashed a muddy handprint onto my leg. I splashed back and then so did she.

The glue had dried, and the coupling was installed. I slowly turned the valve to let the water pressure build. No leaks. We packed up and returned to the shop. Lee walked past as we pulled into the shade of the shop. A look of disapproval crossing his face.

"I'm not even going to ask." He said as he continued, on his way. We were both covered head to toe in the mud. Our playful splashing, quickly turned into a full-on mud bath. I liked to work clean, but once you are dirty, your dirty, so might as well have some fun. We decided that we were too dirty to get home in this state. We were both covered in dry mud. We used the garden hose from the green house to take turns washing the mud off each other. The green house had less water pressure but did a good enough job. The hose used to clean the mowers would have blasted the skin right off our bones. The day was almost over so we went back to the cart, leaving the shop area in search of a good spot to have the sun dry us off.

We went into the unplayable area between the first and eighteenth holes, where all the extra soil and rocks were kept. It was a big area, and you could watch the golfers finish their rounds. The sun felt warm as the hose water evaporated, twenty minutes in the sun and we would be dry enough to go home. Over the next few weeks, we became inseparable. We would spend all day working together, digging holes and fixing pipes. We would have conversations about nothing and make plans for a future that was uncertain. I had just quit my college experience, and she was just about to start hers.

One afternoon on driving back to the shop, our hands accidentally touched on the cart seat. They were stuck together for the rest of the summer. We started to go to the movies every week and spent every waking moment together. I was invited out to wing night to meet some of her friends from high school. I never say no to wing night. We had graduated a few years apart, and went to different schools, so I was not expecting to know any of these people. And I didn't. we walked in holding hands and sat down at the table, having arrived last. We sat next to each other and our hands never let go. It was going to be hard to eat wings with one hand, but we would manage. Sitting around the table were her friends from school, most of them were guys, only a couple of girls. We made up a full table of twelve. The conversation turned into them reminiscing of the good old days back at school. I was having as much fun as I could, with people I didn't know, and who I would probably never see again. The wings were ordered and arrived quickly. I like the saucy wings; Megan got the dry ones.

After we finished our dozen wings, one hand style, she looked over at me and said, "you have some sauce in your beard." And before I could even reach for a napkin, she had a serviette pressed against my lips removing the stray hot sauce. The boys around the table grew silent and stared in our direction.

I made eye contact with one of the slack jawed kids and said, "It's good to be king." Smiling big as she finished washing my face. He was not impressed, I didn't care. I wasn't there to make new friends. Once the bill arrived everyone squared up and we went our own ways. Megan and I drove home, holding hands. As the weeks went on, she became more excited to get out of her parent's house and escape to school in the city of champions.

Chapter 27: Winter Worker

At the end of the season, I had made the decision to quit college and not return to school. I told Lee my plan and he offered me a job to stay and work over the winter. I was thrilled and accepted immediately. Over the next few weeks, I worked on painting the shop. The walls were originally white, but after years of machinery running inside, they were a sticky gross yellow. I had to wash the walls before they could be painted, the years of grease making them unworkable. I used the ladders and stood on the work bench to reach the high spots. The grime off the walls dripping down my elbow as I scrubbed the best I could. It took days to get the walls to a state where they would be ready for the paint. As I was working on the walls, Dave our mechanic was working away on his own projects. We had lots of mowers, and they all need oil changes, new tires, and generally just some minor repairs. As I washed I could here him muttering to himself as he banged away on the aging equipment. Dave was a gruff old guy; his beard was stained yellow from decades of cigarettes. His hands were always cut from working on the machines. The grease from the equipment highlighting the deep cracks in his skin. A wrench skipping off a bolt could bust open a knuckle easily on the unforgiving steel. As the days went by, we would work our tasks, and I would try to stay out of his way. Lee was pushing to have all the walls painted before Christmas, so I was working hard to make that happen. Once the walls were completely washed down, I started on the fresh paint job. With the final coat of paint applied to the walls a few days later, the shop was bright and rejuvenated. Except there was a single spot over the window that looked out into the greenhouse. That spot refused to be covered by the paint. The drywall over the window frame had absorbed so much oil in the previous years that the paint just would not stick. Other than that, the shop space was perfect. The job was completed by the deadline, and I was satisfied with the results. It was a big task, but the finished project looked good.

I had a few days off at Christmas. When I returned Lee called me into his office, I was early, and Dave had not arrived yet. Lee told me to take a seat. I sat in the chair across the desk from him. Lee started "The course has been sold." "Some corporate golf outfit has purchased us." He said with little excitement.

I asked "so, what does that mean for us?"

Lee took a deep breath "Well, at the end of the day I'm going to fire you and Dave." He said in a low voice. I was shocked by this news. Before I could ask any questions, he continued "However, I want you to come back tomorrow, and get rehired." I let out a sigh of relief. "This is giving us a chance to get rid of Dave." He explained. Unbeknownst to me Lee had been looking for a reason to cut Dave loose for awhile and this was the perfect opportunity. "So, when I fire you, get upset." He smirked. "And don't say anything about tomorrow." I nodded with understanding, and waited for the end of the day.

As the day lingered on, the impending doom of being fired clouded my mind. Unsure on how Dave would take the news. As the day ended, Lee called us into his office to break the news of the company purchase and the termination of our services. Dave and I stood there silently, I reached out my hand and thanked Lee for the experience. After a firm, genuine handshake I left.

At dinner that night Dad asked how my day went.

Grinning like an idiot I answered, "I got fired."

A look of shock raced across his face "What!" "Why, what, how?" stammering over all the questions at once. After a moment to compose himself "why are you smiling?"

I told him of the acquisition and that Dave, and I got fired.

"So why are you happy about this?" he asked again.

"I get rehired tomorrow" I explained, "but they are not bringing Dave back." "I don't know why exactly, I didn't ask." A look of relief crossed my fathers face.

"Your lucky" he said shaking a playfully threatening fist in my direction. "You would have had some explaining to do." We all had a chuckle and continued to eat dinner.

I returned to work the following day. Lee and I sat in his office as I filled out some paperwork to get my job back.

After a few moments with an elephant in the room I asked "So, what about Dave." Lee didn't hold back. Evidently Dave was a drunk. He liked to drink all day, every day. He had hidden bottles secretly stashed all over the shop. Over the next few weeks, I found a bunch of them. The last few years I had never noticed his drinking. We never did spend too much time together. Most of the day, the boys were out on the course, so no one would bother him. The last few weeks were the most time I had ever spent near him. Lee explained that all Daves visits to the supply room, next to the office, he would consume his secret bottle of wine. This started to make sense, as I saw Dave going in and out of that small room often. I just assumed that he was getting parts. Lee said that there were warnings given to Dave and he should not have been overly surprised by the events of the previous day. I was relieved to hear that Dave had not taken the termination hard. I was then told that it would be my job to pick up the slack and get everything ready for the new season. I was ready for the challenge.

Over the next few weeks, I was given small tasks to pass the time. I painted the tee box markers. Monday, I painted the red ones, Tuesday the white, Wednesday the blue. Before the paint was even dry, I was at Lee's office door. "What's next?" I would chirp. He would give me another task for the following day, I would complete it, returning to his door "What's next." After a couple of weeks of the "what's next" I had gotten under his skin.

"Ok, fine. Have I got a job for you" he said. "Help me get this mower apart." pointing to the blade reel of the green's mower. We took our time and disassembled the frame from the machine. Pulling out the blade reel. "I'm going to have you sharpen these blades." He explained. "This would take Dave weeks, so it should keep busy for awhile." We took the reel over to the grinder and locked it into the rotating brackets. "All you need to do is slide the grinder across the blade, rotate the reel, and grind the next blade. After that, you tighten this wheel, and it readjusts the grinder towards the blade. Repeat these steps until you have a good, sharp edge on the reel blades." "When you finish this one, we have 11 more to do." I nodded with understanding. Lee walked away with a chuckle as I turned on the grinder. His expectation was that this would take weeks to complete.

I stood in front of the grinder, wearing safety goggles. The headphones from my Walkman blasting the local rock station into my ears. Pushing the switch up, the grinder wheel began to spin. Pulling the rough grinding wheel across the mower blade sent sparks shooting in all directions. The safety glasses were definitely a good idea. The smell of grinding metal quickly filled the room. From left to right I moved the grinder, one, two. Then I would rotate the reel to the next blade, one, two. And again. These reels had eight blades that needed to be sharpened. The idea was that as the reel blades spin, they almost make contact the stationary blade under the frame, and working like scissors, cut the grass with precision. After I had passed the grinding wheel over each of the eight blades, I would tighten the grinding wheel closer and repeat the process. I could see the dull bur of the reel blades start to disappear and be replaced with a blue metal shine from the newly sharpened edge. I found my rhythm. With the music drowning out the noise of the grinder, I worked. Back and forth, over and over. Tightening the wheel. In less than an hour, I had reached a point where I felt that the first reel was complete.

I shut down the grinder, pulled the headphones from my ears, and went over to Lee's office. As I approached Lee barked from his chair

"There is no way you are finished so soon." He chirped.

"I think I might be, can you come have a look?" I stated.

Lee grunted up from his chair, annoyed at the interruption, and certain that the job was completed half assed. He grabbed some paper strips off the desk as he passed through the door. Lee walked up to the reel, placed his paper between the blades and rotated slowly. The paper cut with ease, he slid it down the blade and turned the reel again. He made six cuts along the face of the blade. Small pieces of paper now littered the floor. Stepping back and taking look over at me.

"That's the sharpest I have ever seen those blades." He explained. "How did you do it so fast?" "Dave would have taken a whole day on one of those, and they never turned out that sharp."

I didn't have a secret technique. I explained "I was just giving it the one, two, rotate one two and repeat." He was impressed with the results. We pulled off the reel from the bracket and placed it on the work bench. It was quickly replaced by the next reel, and I went back to grinding. When the set of three reels were all finished, we put them back in the mower frames and reattached them to the green's mower. The whole process for all the bladed machines took just over a week, and the reels had never been sharper.

It was the last Friday that I was going to have to work alone. On Monday the rest of the boys would start work and I was excited to get the team back together. I had planned to go to Edmonton for the weekend to see Meghan. I asked Lee early in the day if I could sneak out early.

"I just need you too dead head all the geraniums in the greenhouse." He instructed. "Then you can get out of here for the weekend." The green house was thirty feet long and filled with geraniums. They had been saved from the previous season, with the intention to be replanted in the spring. I had been watering them for the last few months and they looked like they were growing in mutagen. The bright red flowers were open and bright, the green stems were tall and thick. The winter care had made them strong.

"Thanks Lee, I will get that done no problem," I said.

Leaving the shop and going out to the green house. The moment the greenhouse door opened the humidity and pungent flower smell entered my lungs. The warmth of the room felt good, I immediately removed my jacket. The radio was turned on and the space was filled with the local rock station. With the music blasting, I started on the right side of the room. With a bucket in one hand, and the other reaching out, popping the flowers off each plant. Pop, pop, pop. The bucket was filling up fast. When the bucket was filled to capacity, I found another on the floor. I continued to move systematically down the length of the home-made green house. There were three levels of benches that housed the flowers. The flowers reached out from their pots towards the front of the shelves, trying to absorb the most sunlight as possible. The heads of the flowers were easy to detach. A quick flick of the thumb and the flower fell off. The back wall was shorter than the side walls and I was more than past the halfway point. A wash bason broke up the sidewall that bordered the building, providing a three-foot space that didn't have any flowers. Within less than an hour all the flowers had been removed. The once bright red room was now just green with the stems of the naked plants. I went back into the shop to collect Lee, so he could inspect my work. I then planned on making a hasty departure.

As usual I was greeted with a "You can be done yet?" Lee Said.

"Yep, sure am." I replied, "I didn't miss a single flower!" is said excitedly.

I followed Lee back out to the greenhouse. Lee stepped in and laughed.

"I thought you said you got them all." I chuckled from behind him. Right in the center of the back wall, a single red flower, stood alone, Impossible to miss. "Get out of here" he grumbled. I thanked him and left for the weekend.

Chapter 28: City Of Champions

I spent the weekend in Edmonton and planned to drive home Sunday. Megan and I had a quiet weekend. Spending Saturday at the mall and catching a movie in the theatre. I was excited to get back home on Sunday and planned to leave by midday. On Monday the rest of the team would arrive, and we would start the new season. After lunch Meghan walked me back towards my car. As we approached the area where the car was parked, my stomach dropped. The parking space on the street was empty, and my car was gone. I started to pace along the sidewalk. Looking up and down the street to see if I might have been standing in the wrong location. No such luck the car was gone. Looking at the signage on the street to confirm that there weren't any no parking signs, and there were none. I assumed that the car been stolen. Who wouldn't want to drive a yellow 1987 Camero with a leaky T-top roof. The car had a deep vibration when it started, and I'm sure we would have heard it fire up, even from the 5th floor apartment across the street. We went back upstairs to call the police.

The operator on the phone was polite and understanding, to the urgency that I needed to find my car. I'm sure the operator was accustomed to getting these types of calls and was well equipped to handle all my questions. The keyboard clicked loudly over the phone as the operator entered in my information. With a quick search of my licence plate number, it was determined that the car had not been stolen but had been towed away. I argued that the street did not have any signs instructing to not park there. I was then informed that someone had made a complaint, stating that the car was abandoned, and that's why the car was taken off the street. I was given the address of the impound lot and thanked the operator for her quick resolution to finding the car.

Megan drove me to the impound lot. She parked the car, and we entered the building together, holding hands. The building had the gloomy feeling of the DMV. A few cubicles lined the back of the room. I approached the first teller and was met with pure disdain. I expect that most of the people that come here are not very happy. I gave the teller a smile and her attitude quickly changed. She had her defences up, but I figure you would need to have thick skin working at a place like this. Expecting that most of the people who walk through the door will be grumpy to a certain degree. No one likes going to the DMV.

I rested my hands on the counter and asked politely about my vehicle. She asked for the licence number. I knew it, without having to check. She clicked away on the computer, confirmed that the car was there. All I needed to do was show my licence and proof of insurance. No problem, I keep both of those in my wallet for safe keeping. I pulled out the required information and handed it over. She began to inspect the cards.

Handing them back to me, her expression changed back to being annoyed. "Your insurance has expired" she said. I looked back at her surprised. I took a double look at the insurance card just to make sure and it in fact had expired, on Friday. I stood back from the counter to regroup and plan our next course of action.

Before planning an intricate heist to get my car out of the impound lot, I called back to my house in Calgary to see if any mail arrived on Friday. Mom told me that insurance had arrived earlier in the week and that it was on the counter. I didn't notice it there, so the paperwork never got replaced in my wallet. She suggested that I call the insurance company. I hung up and placed the second call.

My insurance agent answered but told me that the office was not open on Sundays and that the best they could do was fax over a copy of my paperwork on Monday at 9am.

I got the fax number from the grumpy teller and passed it along to the agent.

Looks like I was going to have to spend another night in Edmonton. Megan said she would drive me back to the lot in the morning. Before we left, I called Lee to tell him my predicament.

He laughed and told me not to rush. No need to add a speeding ticket to the misfortune.

I told the teller that "I'll be back", never missing an opportunity to do a terrible impression. We left the small office and returned to Megans apartment for another evening of watching movies and snuggling on the couch. Not a bad trade for a bit of paperwork shenanigans.

The sun was low when we pulled into the parking lot. The impound was due to open any minute. The moment the neon sign started to glow we exited the car. Again, we walked into the building holding hands and approached the counter. The screechy modulation of a fax machine could be heard from behind the counter. I greeted the teller. This was not the same disgruntled person from the day before. Her coffee must have kicked in early because her chipper attitude did not fit the atmosphere. I told her my name and handed over my information, the same as the day before.

Before she could tell me that my insurance expired, I asked her to check the fax that had just screeched on the machine. She turned and collected the page, everything looked good. The transmission had come through nice and clear.

I was then informed that there was a ninety-five-dollar tow fee that I was required to pay before the car would be released. I pulled out my wallet and removed the credit card to pay the fine. There is no way around it, if you want your car back you must pay the fine. There was no use in trying to fight the system of bureaucracy. The paperwork was completed, and my car was being brought to the front but the lot attendant.

I thanked the woman for her quick resolution, and we left the small building. Megan and I exited to the parking lot. We said our goodbyes as my car rumbled into the parking lot. We Embraced passionately for a few short moments, then I got into the idling Camero and started my journey home. Edmonton is 300km from Calgary, so I expected to be home in three hours or less, right in time for lunch.

I had just parked my car and was starching my legs after the long drive from Edmonton, when I could see the caravan of golf carts approaching. I had made it back to the shop in time for lunch. I walked in quickly to see Lee before the others made it into the shop. I was greeted with a smile, as I apologised for being late. I was told not to worry about it, and that I should go have lunch with the boys.

Chapter 29: Straw Removal

I was excited to get back to the course, most of the older kids from last year had planned to move along. I was curious to see who actually returned. This was going to be my season to have some seniority and having the right combination of kids to work with would make the year fun or extremely challenging. Getting back to the shop after lunch Lee handed out pitch forks and asked the team to jump into the back of the two-ton truck. The last few seasons I was still in school for the start of the season. Our first task was to get the straw off the greens. This was a manual labor job and would help build up the team. Nothing like some collective suffering to bring a group of guys together. This was going to be the job for the next few weeks. The straw was laid out over all the greens and some of it would still be frozen in place.

We had a lot of new faces over the next couple of weeks. Some of the boys quit after a few days of heavy lifting. There was one man who had arrived from a Hutterite colony and was only planning to stay for a month anyway. His name was Burt. When we would struggle with the pitch forks, he would effortlessly lift massive stacks into the truck. I would stab the fork into a collected pile of straw and the wooden handle of the pitchfork would flex and creek, with the straw not even coming off the ground. With any more pressure it felt like the pitchfork handle would snap. Burt would walk over, slide his fork into the pile and lift it like it was nothing. It was impressive to see, but I was never able to replicate the results. Each day we would finish cleaning two or three of the greens. I pushed the straw to the edge of the green to make a pile, then stretch to heave it into the truck, really worked out my back muscles. By the time all the greens were cleaned up I was in the best shape of my life. The core strength built by the eight hours of relentless repetitions was unmatched. Once the greens were cleared the rest of the season would be easy because we were all in great shape.

Chapter 30: Range Days

The driving range opened early in the season also. Over the offseason we got to repurpose one of the fairway mowers into a range ball collector and I was excited to see it in action. The cutting blades were replaced with a ball collecting reel. The balls would just fit in between the rows of plastic discs. Then as the trapped balls rotated up, they would hit a pin that would eject them into the regular grass collecting baskets. The reels were able to be raised and lowered the same way as when cutting the grass. When the baskets got full, the arms would be raised, and the machine would be driven back to the range shack. The balls would then be dumped into the ball cleaner to be resold for more practice shots. A driving range is a perfect business. You can sell the same items repeatedly. For five dollars the players got a full basket that contained forty balls. Once all the balls were hit, they would be collected and sold again. It was easy money.

Over the winter I had spent a whole day using the bolt cutters to shape pieces of expanded metal into the patterns needed to armor the fairway unit. Pulling the handles of the bolt cutters together and hearing the snap of the steel was extremely satisfying. Once the steel patterns were cut out, and pieces fitted in place, they would be welded in position by Lee. I made thousands of cuts to the expanded metal that day. Making all sizes and shapes of the grated steel to fully enclose the passenger compartment of the mower. By the end of the day my arms were like jelly from the repetition. Some of the final cuts took both hands to pull the handles together, using my chest as leverage, to snap through the steel. When they day finished, I went home tired. My body was sore, but nothing a hot shower couldn't rejuvenate.

That night, as I was laying in bed trying to sleep. Tossing and turning, unable to find a comfortable position. It happened. A spike of pain ripped across my chest. I had never felt anything like that before. I ran my hands across my ribs. Putting extra pressure on my breastbone, trying to make the pain subside. Nothing was working. I started to panic. Was I having a heart attack? I'm only eighteen, and in pretty good shape. I got out of bed and went upstairs. finding my parents and telling them about my situation. I told them I though I was dying. They looked concerned and took me to the doctor.

We decided that a walk-in clinic would be closer and went there. I was admitted to the doctor immediately and placed in a waiting room. I sat on the paper covered examination table and waited for the doctor to enter. The doctor showed up quickly and I was asked to remove my shirt. The doctor listened to my heart with the ice-cold stethoscope. No irregularities. I breathed a sigh of relief. I was then asked if I had been working out. I said that I have not been. The doctor asked what I did that day? I told him about the bolt cutters and mimicked the movement. The pain shot back across my chest. He could see the pain in my eyes and concluded that this was the cause. Blaming it on micro tears in my muscles. I was a skinny kid and had no extra meat on my bones. I was practically just skin and bone, a walking skeleton. But that was the effect of making that motion for the whole day. Being satisfied that I was not going to die, at least not today, we went home.

The following morning, I woke up and my arms were stiff. My chest felt as if I got punched by a gorilla. I did some quick stretches, and the stiffness disappeared. I went back to work and continued finishing up the steel panels. There were only a few cuts remaining, then the project would be onto the next step. Painting the cage.

The cage was painted a flat black. It matched the original color of the mowers red and black finish. The finished modified mower turned out fantastic. The cage covered all possible entry points for the golf balls to enter. The collection unit was parked out of the way and waited to be delivered when the range opened.

I drove the unit down the path towards the first tee box. I was going to drive the machine on the street to get to the range, and the sidewalk next to the first tee was the only set of traffic lights in the neighborhood where I could cross. I stopped on the sidewalk and waited for my opportunity to cross. It was a three-way intersection, so I would have to wait until all the oncoming traffic had moved before crossing. I found my moment and started to move off the sidewalk. The large front tires bounced as the dropped from the curb. The mower quickly regained composure as I moved down the road. I had about three blocks to drive until I reached the entrance to the driving range. The machine was wider than most road vehicles, so I kept as close to the right-hand sidewalk as possible. Only moving out into the road if a parked car was in my path. The range collector felt slow when being operated on the street. With all the extra space of the world to traverse, it moved along at its maximum speed, but compared to other vehicles it was a snail. The fat tires bouncing with the uneven surface of the road. Knowing the layout of the driving range, I passed by the open gate. If I would have driven the machine into the parking lot, it would have been stuck behind the steel cable barrier and never make it onto the grass. I went further down onto the sidewalk, then drove down a small winding path that stopped just before the range shack. The range attendant was outside moving the golf mats when I arrived. He had a big grin on his face as he walked over to check out the new piece of equipment.

"I can wait to use that." He said with excitement.

"Let me go give it a try, then I can show you all the features." I said. Nodding with excitement, he backed up as I turned the repurposed mower into the range area.

There were a couple of players making use of the range as I crept down the embankment onto the level ground. As I drove down the edge of the range the collector reels were doing a good job of plucking the balls from the ground. The balls rotated as planned in the reels and were dropped into the collection baskets. I got to the far end of the range and made the turn to come back. I lined the machine up with the players, hoping to test out the cage. The players saw my intent, unable to miss the opportunity to hit a moving target they began taking shots. The balls were flying past the cage. My heartbeat racing as the shots got closer. My eyes focusing in on a ball that was hit straight in my direction. My adrenalin spiking as the ball clanged safely off the cage. The steel ringing out after the balls impact. As I approached closer to the players, their accuracy increased and gave the cage a true testing. Multiple shots bouncing off the steel, each one blasting a spike into my pulse. This machine was extremely fun, it also collected the golf balls as intended. I turned back towards the shack and parked the unit. I stepped out of the cage onto the soft ground. My face hurt from the smiling.

"That's really fun when the shots ricochet off the cage." I said. Moving to the front of the machine. I pulled off one of the full baskets of balls. "Where do you want them?" I asked.

The attendant grabbed another basket and said "Right this way." We walked over to the ball wash station that sat tucked behind the shack. The balls roared as they got dumped into the cleaning machine. The balls would jostle around in the cleaning chamber for a few minutes then be pushed out into a wire bin, waiting to be collected into the customer baskets. We walked back over to the collection machine and replaced the buckets. The attendant climbed in, and I gave him a quick tutorial on how the joystick would raise and lower the arms with the buckets. He nodded with understanding and took the machine out to get more balls. I waited around for him to finish collecting the next batch of balls, then I started the walk back to the maintenance shop.

Chapter 31: Dust Storms

As I walked through the gravel parking lot of the driving range, I laughed to myself of all the times I had spent making dust there. I had a yellow Camero, and it was a rear wheel drive. That gave the car the ability to fish tail around corners and make some impressive skid marks. A well-timed pull of the hand break handle and the tires would lock up and squeal. With some precision steering I would make a sharp left turn into the driving range parking lot. The packing lot was made up of gravel and dirt, only the driveway approach was paved. There were fenced in tennis courts on the right side. A cable wire fence, with only a single cable, ran along the other side. The parking area was huge, the golfers would park behind the tee boxes, and the rest of the space was empty.

I stopped in to see my friends who was working at the range shack. We had made plans for that evening, and I was there to pick him up. Working at the shack was an easy job, they would sell tokens to the players, who would get a basket of balls from the machine outside. Players would take hundreds of practice shots, then the balls would be collected and sold again. I always thought that a driving range is a great little business. You are selling a service that can be sold again and again. I drove up slowly to the side of the building and parked. The rumble of the car cutting off as I pulled the key from the ignition. The silence was welcome, as the players tried concentrated on their shots.

I opened the door to the range shack and walked into the small room. There was only a counter at the back, that the employees stood behind, and a small rack of golf gloves off to the side of the window. The shack was made from a trailer and only had the standard single door and a window. The window was covered with expanded metal to prevent the glass from being hit by any stary balls. Mike and Chuck were in there, standing behind the counter, talking about nothing. I was there to get Mike; he was almost finished his shift. Chuck told him he could sneak away early and that he would close the shack for the night. Mike jumped at the chance to go, so we proceeded to leave.

Chuck was the pro golfer at the club house and was the general manager so leaving him behind to lock-up was not a problem, so we left. We got into the car, I turned the key, and the engine roared back to life. I backed out of the parking space slowly and aimed the front end of the vehicle at the exit. A grin crept across my face. Mike noticed the mischievous glint in my eye.

"Don't do it." He pleaded.

My grin grew, as I gripped the steering wheel, pressing on the gas pedal aggressively. The engine roared as the sudden increase of fuel hit the pistons. The rear tires spun, shooting rocks and dirt into the side of the shack. Keeping my foot pressed to the floor, I cranked the wheel to the right. The car began to lose traction and as we went around. The dust billowed into the air as the car spun in a tight circle. This parking lot was the best place to do donuts, and I never missed an opportunity. After about five rotations I could not see the front of the car with all the dust floating in the air. I slowed down and straightened out the vehicle. Once I found my position, I aimed for the exit again, and we made a hasty departure. Looking back into the rear-view mirror I could see a cloud of dust wash over the practicing players. They were not impressed.

"One of these times you're going to get me fired!" Mike said. At this point I didn't work at the course, so I was not overly concerned. As we drove off Chuck looked out the window, watching the dust blow over the angry players on the tee boxes.

Over the next few months every time Mike was working a closing shift Chuck would arrive thirty minutes before the doors were to be locked. Sending Mike home early, or back to the pro shop to run an errand, or some other useless tasks. We were kids and any chance to be off the clock was welcome. Mike never gave the bosses instructions to leave a second thought. However, the others at the pro shop must have felt like something strange was going on. The numbers were weird and weren't adding up. We were completely oblivious to the trickery that was taking place, when Mike was sent away. It was only after the police got involved, that we become wise to the corruption working in the shadows.

Chuck had lived a couple of houses up the hill from my family. He had lived in that corner house for years, and I never even noticed him. The police had gotten a tip, and the investigation had led them to Chuck's door. They knocked, no answer. When they finally forced entry, the house was empty. The entire house was cleaned out, nothing remained. Chuck must have known that law enforcement was on his trail and packed up and moved on in the middle of the night. My mother was nosey and would have noticed a moving truck in the middle of the day. The gossip spread through the neighbourhood like wildfire. Not knowing exactly what Chuck had done, speculation ran wild. There were all kinds of rumors. But the fact remained that he was gone and not able to set the record straight for himself.

After a few months the rumor mill started up again. Claims that come in that Chuck had been apprehended in Vancouver. After the arrest the story goes that he was taking money from the golf course. Every time he would send Mike home early, Chuck would supposedly take money from the till. The same thing was happening at the pro shop. The cash totals every night never added up correctly. It took the accountants months to notice the discrepancy in the records, but it didn't take long to find the suspected culprit. Chuck being the general manager must have been in on the meetings about the missing money. He would have known when it was the right time to make a run for it. Mike was never even suspected as being the perpetrator, his schedule was all over the place, and the thefts were consistent every week. Rumor has it that Chuck had put over a hundred thousand dollars in his pockets over the years. No official report had ever made it back to Lee's desk, but Chuck would be looking at possibly doing some jail time over his sticky fingers. But again, who knows maybe he just moved away, and the people that knew his plans never set the story straight. Everybody loves a villain and a good bit of gossip.

Chapter 32: The Little Tipster

There was an old farm truck sitting unused in the yard. Covered in years of dirt and grime. One morning I was instructed to clean it up, as it had been given a new purpose. I opened the truck door and was met with the smell of the old upholstery. The truck started up with ease, so I drove it over to the wash hose. After giving the truck a blast of water, it's shiny paint gleamed in the sunshine. Hiding under all the dirt was a beautiful deep blue paint with a silver sparkle, almost like the paint of a new boat. A few hours later the truck was picked up and taken away to be modified.

A week had passed, and the blue truck was returned to the yard. It had been retrofitted with a hydraulic dump in the truck bed. The driver had control to raise the back with a small lever that was bolted onto the dash. On the side of the truck were some new decals. The big letters read "Lil tipster." From that moment on the blue truck was referred to as the tipster. Having the capability to haul a load of dirt or sand and dumping it in place would save hours of tiny loads with the carts.

Our first task with the tipster was to refill all the sand traps. The volume of sand in the traps had eroded over the years and were now more like rock pits than sand traps. Drew and I went out to the dumping grounds to get a load of sand. I waited in the truck as he used the bobcat to load up the back. Drew was trained on the bobcat and was the only one authorized to use it. Rather than wait around for my return, he rode with me to drop off the sand. As we approached the first tunnel between the third and forth holes, I didn't slow down. The tunnel was a one-piece concrete construction that went under the neighborhood street. It was basically a square with cut corners, giving it more width than it appeared to have. The truck mirrors raced past the sides of the tunnel, with inches to spare. It was the lucky tunnel after all. The tipster had a manual transmission, and never really had the chance to get past third gear as it always traveled on the course. Drew and I were on our way to the first sand trap of the project. We approached the fourth hole, looking up the long fairway, I geared up. The morning air was crisp, and we were the only ones out on the course. The first golfers wouldn't start for another twenty minutes. The tipster reached 50km, I shifted. The tipster reached 80km, I shifted again. The tipster reached 100km. We had travelled up the fairway in record time, a new land speed record for the fourth hole. Pressing on the breaks as we reached the top of the hill, returning to a comfortable speed of 20km. If there were any homeowners eating breakfast looking out to the course, I'm sure they would have been impressed by the blue flash that zoomed up the grass. There were no official speed limits on the course, but I'm sure we were well over what would have been deemed acceptable. Arriving to the fifth hole in record time we dumped out the sand. The dump mechanism lifting the load with ease, the sand poured out into a tidy pile on the edge of the bunker. As the tipster deck lowered back into position, the rest of the crew arrived. They would adjust the pile of sand in the bunker as we went to get a second load. Each sand trap would need at least three or four loads of sand to get back up to standards. This was going to take a few days to complete. When all the traps were finished, they look like a beach with soft sand.

Chapter 33: Sand Traps

After the traps were rejuvenated, they would to be raked every morning. This would be done while riding on a 3-wheeled ATV. It was setup with a row of spiked bolts and steel fins, designed to breakup the lumps then smooth out the sand into a tidy, uniformed surface. This machine was fun to use. Having the ability to make an incredibly tight turning radius. The unit would make the sharp turns of the sand trap shapes with ease. The handle on the right side of the seat when pulled back would raise the fins. When the handle was pushed forward the breaker bars would drop into the sand. I would start each trap by driving the perimeter and working towards the center. Making the back fin overlap on each rotation to prevent any ridges. I would continue with as many passes as each trap required. Some of the traps were tiny and others would take minutes to complete. When exiting the sand trap there might be some tracks left behind if the fins were lifted too soon. Using the sand rake that was left at every trap I would smooth out any of the final imperfections.

On days after a heavy rain some of the sand traps would be unintentionally filled with water. If there was a puddle in the sand it would be ignored, the water would just evaporate naturally over the day. However, if there was deep water in the sand traps, I would need to pump them out. Once all the traps had been raked, I would know where all the problem spots were located. I would go back to the maintenance shop clean off the trap unit, so that it would be ready for the next day and collect the generator and pump.

Pumping out the traps was a job that would only happen every now and then. Most of the time it would be the same traps that would be filled after a good storm. The generator was more awkward than heavy. It was encased in a square frame that made it easy to get hold of. I would unload it off the cart and leave it next to the flooded sand traps. The generator had to be close enough for the power cord of the pump to reach. The pump would be placed in the water after I attached the large blue water hose to it. I would roll out the hose in a direction that was away from where the foot traffic of the players would go. Usually, it would be aimed towards one of the nearby water hazards. The pullcord on the generator was recently repaired and after a few pulls the unit rumbled to life. The pump immediately started to suck the water from the sand trap. The water flowed down the blue hose. I could see the water expanding the hose as it pushed its way to the far end, bleeding out onto the grass. The water level in the sand was dropping fast, I could see the watermark shrink from the traps edge, as the water was relocated. Once most of the water was moved, I would stop the pump and dig a hole in the sand. All the remaining water would rush to fill the newly opened space. I would drop the pump back into the new hole and have it suck out the remainder of the water. Once the trap was free of the excess rainfall, I would reload the generator and pump into the cart. I would then rake the trap and move onto the next puddle that needed to be relocated.

Chapter 34: Fertilizer Run

Drew and I were sent to the UFA to pickup thirty-six bags of fertilizer. Two bags would be used on each green. Once every year the greens would be aerated and fertilized. This was done early in the season, when there was rain in the forecast. An early application of fertilizer gave the short grass the best chance to grow strong over the season. We arrived at the UFA and our order was ready for pickup. We had driven over in the little tipster truck. The decals on the side and its hydraulic dump bed turned heads on our arrival. The other farmers had some questions about the addition to the truck, and how well it worked. After giving a quick positive product review Drew and I started to load the 50lb bags into the back of the truck. Drew was on the ground handing the bags up to me. I was standing in the truck bed, stacking the bags neatly, so that we would have enough space for all of them to fit. The bags were heavy enough, but not unmanageable, just awkward. We were taking our time loading the truck when a farmer walked over.

"Hey boys, let me give you a hand," he said.

The farmer was wearing a plaid shirt and coveralls, he had a friendly grin on his face. As I looked down from the truck at our new helper, I noticed that he only had one arm. Before we even had time to accept his offer, he grabbed the next 50lb bag with his large hand and lifted it up and into the truck like it was nothing. We were down to our last few bags, and he pitched them into the back of the truck like they were feather pillows.

He grinned and as he walked away said "Now, that how you load a truck Boys."

We thanked him as he walked out of view. Drew and I looked at each other in amazement at the man's power. I jumped off the back of the truck, closed the tailgate, and we drove back to the shop.

Parking the truck at the shop with the tail gate pointing into the open garage door, I called over the others to help us unload all the bags of fertilizer. There was a small room in the corner that housed all the fertilizers and other chemicals that were used around the course. The room only had a normal sized door, so we would need to move the bags one at a time into the room. The bags would be put in there until they were needed. It was a safe, dry space. As the others helped to move the bags from the truck to the storage room, I challenged them to only use one hand. Telling the story of the strong man who helped us at the UFA. I was only able to get the bag off the ground with one hand, but there was no way I could have lifted it into the truck bed. The man was truly impressive. The others tried, and some couldn't even move the bag from the floor. It was a "sword in the stone" moment as we all tried our best to lift the bags. Giving even more prestige to the legend of the one-armed man.

The next day we started the aeration of the greens. It took all day, as the hole punch machine only had one speed. Slow. How slow? It was like walking a dead dog. The machine would propel itself forward at a snail's pace, punching a row of holes. The holes would then be removed from the ground and leave behind a pile of dirt stumps, they looked like dog turds. I had used the machine the year before and was not enthusiastic to be the operator this year, so I let one of the others take it out. Whoever was not operating the aeration machine would push snow shovels across the green, consolidating all the plugs. The plugs would then be scooped into the small trailer used to haul the daily grass clippings. The aeration team would get a three-hole head start, and then be followed by the fertilizer team. A golf cart would be loaded with as many bags of fertilizer as it could carry and follow around the fertilizer spreader.

I was operating the fertilizer spreader this year. The fertilizer machine had a hopper on the front and would be filled with the multicolored fertilizer pellets. The hopper would take almost an entire bag of fertilizer. As the little beads of grass nutrition hit the ground they would be brushed into the newly formed rows of holes. The fertilizer would bounce all over, landing on the machine and the operator. I blame this on my thick hair, the stray fertilizer giving extra nutrition to my skull. When the cart was down to the last of the bags, the fertilizer would be unloaded onto the side of the green. The cart driver then would race back to the shop to reload. Aiming to meet the fertilizer machine at the next hole, while stopping to pickup the empty bags on the way. The cart driver would have to be careful to not overload the cart with the fertilizer bags. If the back box was too full, the front wheels would leave the ground, and the cart would be unable to steer. Eight bags seemed to be the magic number. There was enough weight in the back to barely keep the wheels on the ground. Each green took two bags, so they would make the trip back and forth until all the bags were distributed. As soon as all the fertilizer bags were delivered, the driver would go and collect the full trailer with the grass plugs. When arriving back at a green that was still covered in plugs, the delivery driver would step in to help, until the green was finished, then they would remove the trailer. Everyone did their part, and no one complained. We were a well-organized group and got the job done. This was the only job that was time sensitive. It needed to be completed in a single day. If we needed to stay past our normal work hours, so be it. All the plugs needed to be removed before we went home. This task always ran late, and we were rewarded with a pizza dinner, to keep us energized.

These were always long days. In previous years I had been on the shovel crew. Looking back that was probably the best of the tasks. The aerator was slow moving, and not as fun to operate as it looked. The fertilizer spreader was a rough ride, bouncing between the greens, and you spent the whole day alone. The shovel crew however was six of the boys, talking trash all day. There were not too many days where we all got to work together, so this was always a treat. The day was spent pushing shovels, sure, but the banter made the time go faster. The fertilizer spreader would almost always catch up to the aeration crew, burning up the three-hole lead they started with. Shoveling the plugs off the green was more time consuming than expected. The morning gusto faded away as the day wore on. When the last green was punched, and the plugs were being collected the boys were moving slow. Pushing the shovels all day had taken a toll. We would all go home stiff and sore from a hard day's work. Dreaming of hot showers to knock the stiffness from our bodies.

Chapter 35: The First Saturday in April

Spring had arrived early in the year 2000. The golf bug had bitten my parents hard. The course was calling to them. They liked to play an early game, starting around 9am. This would give them the rest of the day for normal weekend errands after the round. At some point over the winter my dad had purchased himself a new driver, and he was excited to try it out. This club was the future of golf, "The ball smasher 2000". It was advertised to hit the ball farther and with more precision than any other club previously designed. It was made from space age materials that were used on the rockets that got launched into space. Dad had been doing some serious trash talking all week on how this would be the ultimate equalizer to his game. Now that he had the ball smasher, he would be unstoppable. For the record my mom was undefeated for the whole last season. The last time my dad scored less than my mother was the day she got a hole in one. The best part of that was the score card was framed and hung on the family room wall as a trophy. Which was a bitter-sweet reminder of both their achievements.

My parent had gotten to the course early and checked in. They went over to the first tee box to wait their turn. The group ahead of them had made their first shots and were moving down the fairway. My parent's group waited for the other players to get out of sight, then took their spots on the tee box. Dad waited for the other players to make their tee shots first. All the other balls bounced and rolled down the fairway respectable distances. Mom had a great shot that landed in the middle of the fairway. It was now time for him to show the world how this new club was going to blast his shots further than ever before. Dad approached the tee box, removing the club cover as he walked. Stopping dead in his tracks, his heart sank. His body became hot with anger as he raised his fist to the sky and cursed my name.

Earlier in the week Dad had been in the workshop cleaning his clubs and changing the spikes in his and my mothers golf shoes. He replaced any of the marked or damaged balls with new ones. Making sure to have the golf bags fully stocked with new tees and fresh towels. His excitement for the first game of the season filled the room. Once his bag was ready for action, he left it by the back door, waiting until it was time to put into the trunk of his car. The unattended bag was an easy target for some shenanigans. Not being able to pass up a prime opportunity to play a trick on my father, I sprang into action. Next to the furnace were all the old golf clubs from ages past. I walked into the dimly lit space and pulled a number one driver out of the dusty leather golf bag. I took it over to Dad's freshly organized golf bag and made the switch. I rushed the traded club back to the leather bag before anyone would notice the mix-up. I did not expect anyone to inspect both the leather bag and the newly organized clubs before the game on Saturday. A short while later Dad moved the clubs from the back door to the trunk of his car, where they would wait safely until the anticipated match on the weekend.

With a cocky stride my father approached the tee box. Removing the cover from his super weapon of a club. He pulled the cover off expecting to see the shine of space age material, his eyes were met with the dull bronze of days gone by. His body filled with a hot anger, as he looked around for the culprit. I was nowhere to be found. With the others looking at him with confusion, as he stormed around the tee box. Then once they noticed the club in his hand, laughter erupted. The "ball smasher 2000" was replaced with a "POS 1922". The old club was a relic of a simpler time when "woods" were actually made from wood. This was not going to be the game he had expected to play. Dad's eyes darted around, refusing to admit defeat. His expectations of me appearing shrinking by the moment. I was not there to return the driver. After the composure returned to the group, He accepted defeat and played his first shot. Not happy about the trickery that had just occurred. For the rest of the round Dad had the expectation of me popping out of a bush or bunker to return his club. That was not going to happen. The joke was set and that was that. I had been home for a few hours at this point, after completing my weekend tasks at the course.

Just after lunch I could hear the garage door opening. A car door closed, rather forcefully, with a loud echo. Dad bursts into the house and was greeted by me, grinning like an idiot, holding back laughter.

"April fools," I proclaimed, "how was your game?"

A flicker of fire shot through his eyes. A smirk started to grow on his lips. "You got me good," he conceded. "When did you make the switch?" he asked.

"Mid week after you cleaned them up." I told him.

"Where is it?" he asked.

"In the furnace room." I told him.

He went and collected his super club from the old leather bag, removed the ancient head cover. Made a double check and walked back into the garage to put the club back into its rightful place. For the rest of the season Dad checked his bag every time before he left to play.

Chapter 36: The Side Hustle

Megan only worked at the course for a single season. She was going to school in Edmonton taking all horticultural classes. Her first year had finished and she was returning home for summer employment. She got a job working at a yard renovation place. Her task was to draw out possible landscapes for clients. Utilizing her newfound knowledge of the best plants for the required environments. Knowing which plants would survive best in direct sunlight, over plants that preferred the shade. On the weekends I would help with the yard projects that she booked during the week. Her job on the weekdays was to draw up the yard plans and, on the weekends, turn them into reality. I was happy to help, as we got to spent time together, and some extra money didn't hurt.

One Saturday Megan was running late. I was asked to start the job, and she would arrive shortly after nine. I pulled up to the address provided, the Camero's rumble shaking the street. The morning air was still crisp as the clock turned nine. I was right on schedule. I stepped out of the car; a pile of rocks and a pile of dirt were placed on the driveway a few houses down. I started to walk over to the yard, wanting to get a good look at the space we were going transform. The front door of the house opened, and the homeowner rushes outside. Expecting to be greeted with a friendly good morning I extended my arm for a handshake.

"Your late." The man barked.

I lowered my arm, confused by the hostility. "How do you mean?" I asked puzzled.

"You were supposed to be here at 830." The man grumbled.

I don't deal with hostility well in the mornings. "Well, I got here as soon as I could." I tried to explain.

"Being late is unacceptable." The man complained. I cut him off before he could start his lecture on tardiness.

"Hey man, I was at my job at 630 working on the golf course cutting the greens, and your lucky I'm here at all." This stopped him in his tracks. I could hear Megan's car being parked, and she arrived quickly.

"Good morning, sorry I'm late." She said with a cheery greeting, standing by my side. The mans demeanor changed and he became welcoming.

We walked around the yard and planned out the day. Where the dirt was to be spread out. How the rocks would form the path from the side of the house out to the tree in the yard. The goal for the day was to get all the groundwork finished, then on Sunday Meagan would come back and plant all the foliage in the newly constructed flower beds. This was not our first weekend of the side hustle and completion of the job was going to be easily done by sundown.

We unloaded the tools from our vehicles and started to move the dirt into place. I made no mention of the man's early morning bad attitude and didn't give it a second thought. As the day progressed the pile of dirt disappeared off the driveway, being distributed into the flowerbed under the front window of the house. The flowerbed was reshaped under the window to have a larger curve in the front, then transition up to the front steps. The rocks were moving slowly, but the curved path was starting to take shape. The afternoon sun was getting hot. The wife of the house stepped out with a pitcher of ice-cold lemonade and that was greatly appreciated. The refreshments reinvigorated the landscape efforts as we pushed on to finish the job.

The yard looked good. All the soil and rocks were moved into their new positions as planned. The man walked out onto the driveway to admire the completed project. Approaching me with an extended arm, I was met with a firm handshake. Then I was surprisingly pulled in for a short, yet strong hug. Looking over the man's shoulder I could see his teenage son looking out the front window, envious of the affection.

"Sorry about this morning." The man apologized. "I thought you were just another lazy teenager."

"No worries, I thought you were just another grumpy old man." I said with a grin. He laughed and thanked us for our hard work. I finished loading up the tools, as Megan was getting paid for the day. I didn't mind the extra work; she was fair with the pay. It was more than I was getting paid at the course. Some of the weekends I would have the time overlap and be getting double pay. The summer was short, so we tried to do as many extra jobs as possible. Megan had another yard scheduled for the following weekend.

I got a call from Megan in the middle of the week. she was upset.

"what's wrong?" I asked with concern.

"I got fired from my job" she wept.

"How did that happen?" I asked again.

Unbeknownst to me, Megan had been making up the quote proposals for the company she was working for. When a customer would complain about the cost, she would tell them that she would be capable of doing the project for less and undercut the company she was working for. When her boss found out about this betrayal, she was fired on the spot. And rightfully so. This was dirty and underhanded. I was surprised when she told me of her corruption. Evidently the grumpy old man from the weekend before had called in to complement on our good work. This call of praise opened a can of worms, as the boss had no idea of the job he was speaking of. Once Megan was confronted with questions about the weekend jobs, she confessed to the poaching of clients and her employment was terminated. This would be the start of the decline our relationship. I hold trust and loyalty to the highest standard, and her lack of respect for her boss spoke volumes about her character.

As the summer ended, I enjoyed not working every waking hour. Megan was going back to Edmonton to finish her next year classes. We started to grow distant. Her first visit back to town was thanksgiving. She had brought a "friend" from Edmonton to stay with her family for the weekend. I knew I had been replaced. We broke up and I moved on.

Chapter 37: Grumpy Old Men

I arrived at the shop before sunrise. Lee was sitting in his office looking worried. I went in and took my regular seat. He looked up from the news paper that was spread across his desk.

"I need you to take me to an appointment this morning" Lee requested.

"No problem, what time do you need to be there?" I asked.

"We should leave here around eight." he suggested.

"Ok, then. I will be back here for before eight." I didn't ask more questions and left to get my task completed before our departure. I had planned to move the holes, so I rushed to get them all relocated.

At eight o'clock we were climbing into his truck.

"Where are we going?" I asked, stepping up into the driver's seat. The smell of the dusty old truck filling my lungs. Over the last few weeks, I had been given the honor of driving Lee's truck, and had become comfortable in its musk.

"I have a doctor's appointment in the tall building over by the mall." He said.

"I know where that is," I said confidently "We have family dinners over there all the time."

Lee looked over at me with uncertainty in his eyes. I couldn't tell if he was not confident in my navigation to the mall or what the doctor visit would reveal. As we got onto the main road Lee started squirming in his seat.

"Are you all right?" I asked with concern.

"I'm fine, I just had to drink a bunch of water before the appointment." "They are planning on running some tests and I needed to be hydrated" he explained.

As we got closer to the destination his discomfort grew. I parked the truck close to the front doors and we both got out. I followed Lee into the doctor's office and took a seat while he checked himself in. He returned quickly and took a seat next to me.

"She doesn't think it won't be much of a wait." He said, gesturing up at the nurse behind the counter.

As I looked around the room, I was the youngest person in the waiting area by decades. The room was filled with ten old men, all squirming in their chairs. Some waiting more patently than others. One of the old guys creaked out of his chair and waddled up to the reception desk. His conversation was muffled but he was clearly agitated. After a brief interaction with the nurse, she pointed him back to his seat. He returned without conflict, defeated. Another grey-haired gentleman got up and marched over to the desk. His voice elevated with urgency,

"I need to use the rest room." He exclaimed.

"You're going to have to wait," the nurse instructed.

"If you don't want to see a puddle on the floor, I'm gonna need to use the washroom." The man barked back with urgency in his voice. His weight shifting from one foot to the other. It was the unmistakable pee your pants dance.

"Please go sit down, the doctor will be right with you." The nurse directed.

"Please, just a few drops." The man pleaded.

"Go take a seat!" the nurse pointed over to the chair.

The man turned and retreated to his seat, resting back down with a grown. His discomfort clearly visible. The room was filled with a group of old men all trying their absolute best to not wet their pants.

The doctor soon arrived and took in the first patient. Every two minutes after that the doctor would appear and remove another squirming old man from the waiting room. Eventually it was Lees turn and he exited the area with obvious discomfort. I sat alone in the waiting room for awhile. Looking around the room, the art on the walls were framed with the brass trim that was popular at the time. The art inside the frames were dull and uninspired. The carpet was a worn out in in front of the reception desk. There were magazines on the small table in the corner of the room, none of them were current. The magazine pile was messy and unorganized. I could hear the nurse shuffling papers behind the desk, but I couldn't see her. The chairs sat low; I was unable to see over the tall counter. I sat quietly and waited. After a while, the old men started to reappear into the waiting area. Each one of them stopped at the desk and gave the nurse a courteous goodbye. Some stayed longer to make their next appointment. They all arrived back in the waiting area in the same order as they had been originally called. I started to count down to when I expected Lee to emerge from the back rooms.

Lee walked out from the back office and approached the desk to make the next appointment. I waited until he turned and stepping away from the desk before I stood up and followed him out the door. We got into his truck, and I put the key in the ignition.

"How did it go?" I asked.

"I should have some results back in a week or so." Lee said with a hint of fear in his voice. Waiting for results is the absolute worst. Your mind runs all the worst possible scenarios. Its easy to fall into an emotional spiral of doubt and fear. Its hard to make, a plan of action if you don't have any details to start from.

"I'm sure you will be fine." I said with encouragement. We drove back to work. Lee sat in the passenger seat silently, worried about the test results.

The following week, Lee got a call from the doctor's office, and the news was terrible. The doctor broke it down as a good news, bad news situation. Trying to make the bad news easier to handle. Bad news was Lee had prostate cancer. The good news was that it was in the early stages, and with rapid treatment it could be defeated. Lee had a good positive attitude towards the treatments and got started right away. I would drive him to his appointments as required. The day after a treatment Lee was in a weakened state and would stay home from work to recover.

When Lee was away from the course I was left in charge. I knew what needed to be done and the boys didn't push back against my directions. I remembered the lessons of the past and didn't let the perceived authority go to my head. I was the one with most seniority, so they did what I asked without many questions. They all knew that I would do the same tasks if required. Drew was my second in command. I would be good cop, he would play bad cop. If I needed an attitude adjusted Drew would apply the pressure to get the required results. His skills at being the hammer were not needed every day, but on occasion they were required. I had done this job for three years at this point, the routine had become second nature. There was still time to play around, but the work needed to be finished. I had learned all my leadership skills from Lee and was determined to be a "follow me boys" type of leader. Rather than just some asshole that sat in the office and barked out orders. So, I spent most of the days out on the course working side by side with the others.

Chapter 38: The Mole 2000

Arriving to the shop first was one of my favourite times of day. The stillness of the empty building was refreshing to the chaos that the day had potential to bring. I unlocked the door and walked in. My hand reaching for the alarm keypad out of habit. My index finger extended to press the code ready silence the low tone of the panel. However, the panel was already silent. The lights were already on. This was strange. The shop was dark when I left the day before. I took a few steps forward, into the main area of the building. Standing at the far end of the work bench was a tall man holding a coffee.

"Good morning." He greeted me with a smile.

"Who are you, and how did you get in here?" I asked firmly. It was too early in the day for a conflict, I was not awake enough for this.

"Today is my first day, I'm Blair." He explained.

I asked again "How did you get in here?"

He raised a key "I got this from Lanny."

I was not impressed. Lee had only been away for a few days and the pro shop was already sticking their nose into our business.

I walked over and took the key, "You won't be needing that." I said, sliding the key into my pocket. "What are you expecting to do here?" I asked.

Blair thought about it for a second and responded with "I'm just here to help, I can do whatever needs to be done."

"Fantastic, we got lots to do." I said, with a hint of sarcasm in my voice.

There was no need to be rude, but I wanted to let him know that I was not impressed by his presence. The rest of the team was starting to arrive. Blair stood to the back and greeted the others with a timid smile and raised hand. We all gathered in the lunchroom and got ready for the day. Just as we were ready to leave and get the day going, Lanny showed up. He walked into the shop; I could hear his fancy shoes clacking on the concrete. Lanny stood in front of Lee's office door. Looking over the team, he started to give out orders.

Pointing at the boys, "You can cut the fairways, you can cut the rough, 14 needs a fence trim." He stopped.

No one even acknowledged his commands. Nobody moved. You could have heard a mouse fart, and maybe he did. Lanny stood there with a look of surprise on his face, and with the posture of "don't you know who I am." They were all looking at me. By this time in the season, we were a well-oiled machine. We all knew what needed to be done and who was going to do what. I looked over to the boys and straightened out the tasks. Sending them off to get started.

"When you finish all that, we can get out to 14." I added.

There was no harm in doing what was asked, but it was who and how it was asked that was the problem. As the last of the boys left the shop, it was just Lanny, Blair and me. I looked at Lanny, then over to Blair.

"We don't need a babysitter with Lee away." I started "I don't appreciate a new person in the shop before I even get here."

Lanny looked stunned that I was not folding under his direction. Lanny was in charge of the front end; Lee was the boss out here. The pro shop would run and hide at Lanny's approach and jump any time he demanded.

"And I only take my orders from Lee." "We have a weekly schedule that we follow, and don't require your instructions, we have this under control." I stated firmly.

My patience was being tested, and it was still too early for this.

"Alright then." Lanny conceded and left the shop.

Blair and I were left staring at each other.

I broke the silence "Alright then." I mimicked "lets get you the tour and figure out the day."

Blair was receptive to my distain for Lanny, but I was not going to blindly trust Blair, but he was going to be with us, so we may as well do some work. We jumped in a cart and started out to do a lap around the course. Blair was probably twenty years older than me, late thirties, he explained how he was retired and just looking for something to do. He had sold his business and had money in the bank, so the wage for cutting the grass was not his concern. He was happy with the perk of getting free golf as an employee and planned to exploit it at every opportunity.

He was not a bad guy, we just got off to a rough start. If he would have been standing at the door waiting for me, and not inside, I would have had no reason not to trust him. We finished the tour and went back to the shop; I pointed him to the whips and sent him back out to 14 to clean up the fence line. He had to pay some dues, everyone had to use the whips, it was a right of passage. If he was going to fit in, he was going to have to work for it.

At the end of the day, I was the last one out of the yard. I stopped my car just outside the gate so it could be closed and locked. I got out and put the chain around the bars, clicking the lock shut. I got back in the car and drove towards the club house. As I passed by, I looked over into the parking lot and I could see Blair's truck parked on the decorative bricks, close to the front door. He went straight from the shop to the club house to report back on his day. I was not worried. We had a productive day and tried to include him in the work. We had our fun, but the work always got done. Over the next few weeks, we got more comfortable with Blair around and things went back to normal. He did report back to the club house at the end of every day and was not to be fully trusted.

Chapter 39: The Return of Blair

Blair was the mole. There was no denying it. He was sent into spy and make sure that we did what was expected of us. This deception was easy to spot, so we just went on with the regular business. We had nothing to hide.

Blair ended up being not a bad guy. He had recently sold a business and got a ridiculously good price for it. He was only working for the entertainment, and the free golf. We got to play free if we worked at the course. This included the maintenance team. I never took full advantage of the perk, who wants to spend four more hours at work after a hard day. Not me. Blair was excited to use the course on his off hours and had made great improvements in his game. He was a basketball fan, and the closest professional team was in Vancouver. Blair would never work on weekends and when he would return Mondays he had stories from his trips to Vancouver. I never questioned the validity of the stories, I didn't care. He would tell us how he got on a flight, went to the game, then flew home. If he had the money and wanted to travel a province over to watch a basketball game, why not. Blair finished out the season with us. Reporting back to the pro shop on our daily activities. I didn't expect his reports to be very exciting, we were behaving for the most part.

Blair returned the following season and was greeted with less contempt than the previous year. He had earned enough respect so that on his return the title of mole was dropped. One morning Blair arrived and was more excited than normal. He told me that his neighbor was hired and that she was going to start next week.

"Wait to you see her" he beamed. "She is gonna out work all of you." He bragged.

I didn't get too excited. In true fashion we would wait for a few weeks to see what she was truly made of. He went on to tell us that she rode horses and was really tough. She was going to be placed on the horticulture team and help with the maintenance of the flower beds.

Erin arrived on the next Monday and went to work in the greenhouse. She spent the day in there working on the flowerpots. It was cold and fresh in the mornings, so she was wearing a toque, and I was not able to get a good look at her. As the day progressed the boys all lingered around the shop hoping to get a peak. Blair had talked her up, so we wanted to see if she would live up to the hype.

I had finished using the fairway mower and was washing off the grass clipping, and I finally had a sighting. She was driving back from the pro shop, her long blonde hair blowing in the wind. As she drove past, I turned off the hose, not wanting to inadvertently spray her with splashing water from the mower. She had a warm inviting smile as she drove away. I finished up washing down the mower and parked it in the sunshine to dry. I walked over to the greenhouse to make a proper introduction. She was cute and kind of funny, and that piqued my interest. We chatted for awhile about nothing and waited for the day to end.

We walked over to our vehicles at the end of the day. I drove a yellow Camaro; she drove a white mustang.

After of few weeks of flirty conversations we decided to go to the movies and grab some dinner. At the end of the day, she wrote her phone number on the palm of my hand. I drove home to get cleaned up. I then planned to give her a call to work out the details of our date. I rushed into the house to find some paper and a pen so that I could transcribe the number down. My hear sank, the last two numbers had smudged off my palm on the three-minute drive home. I wrote down the five legible numbers and went for my shower. Making the calculations in my head as I washed off the grime of the day. There were only 99 possibilities.

Once I was cleaned up and re-dressed, I started calling numbers. It was excruciating, each call had the anticipation and hope of talking with my new crush. Each number brough in a new disappointment with a failed "sorry, wrong number." Until I finally hit the right combination, and her familiar voice answered. Refilled with excitement, we made our plans and went out on our first date. We then spent the rest of the summer together, hanging out and going to the movies.

One day Erin and I were working together over on hole fourteen. It was the end of the day, and we were going back to the shop. She was driving the cart along the edge of the fairway. There was a path that had started to form between the trees, so we tried to avoid it. She cranked the wheel to the right; the cart took a sharp turn off the newly formed path, back onto the fairway. We were moving too fast, and to avoid a tree she cranked the cart back to the left. The slight incline of the ground mixed with the quick direction change lifted the carts wheels off the ground. Unable to recontrol the cart, it started to roll over. I was tossed from the cart and landed on the grass. Laying on my back looking up at the sky. It's as if time slowed down, the cart was still rolling over and I was underneath it. I watched as the bottom of the cart turned and began to fall on top of me. In those short seconds, my mind had time to prepare for the accident. I expected pain and braced for the impact. The cart came to rest on top of me. I felt nothing, no pain, no pressure, nothing. I sat up and the cart rolled off. I must have been tossed from the cart on the first maneuver. I was sitting on the ground dazed by our accident; Erin ran over and jammed her thumb into my forehead.

Pulling her hand back she exclaimed "your, bleeding."

By now the golfers who had been on the tee box had rushed over to make sure everyone was alright. I had a small cut along my hairline in the center of my forehead. I gathered my self and stood up. Looking around at the scene of the rollover. All the contents from the cart were dumped out onto the grass. I was in shock and went into robot mode, picking up the debris from the ground and putting it back in the cart. All the while providing assurance that I was alright. A small trickle of blood dripping down my face. We collected all the stuff off the ground and got back in the cart. Erin got back behind the steering wheel and drove us carefully back to the shop.

The ride back was a blur, but mostly her apologizing for the accident. I'm not one to worry about what ifs, so I was alright and there was nothing more to worry about. We got back to the shop, and I went into the washroom to see in the mirror the extent of my head injury. I ran the water until it got warm, then washed my face with my hands. I had a small cut, nothing really, it was in my hairline and when it scared would be unnoticed. We finished up the day and I went home.

I showed my mom the new damage I had received. Not telling her exactly how it had happened. I blamed it on a stray branch whacking me in the face. I didn't want her to worry about what really happened. It could have been way worse. The cart was full of rebar and rope that we use to mark out holes that we dig. It would have been very possible to have been impaled by one of the rebars as the cart rolled. But lucky enough that was not the case.

Over the next few months, the head wound would spontaneously start to bleed for no reason. I would just be out with friends and a trickle of blood would slide down my face. A quick wipe and a guarantee that I was alright and we were back to normal.

Chapter 40: Weakness for Puddles

It was time for a break. I drove back to the shop and walked in the side door. Parking my cart in the shade of the building. The sun was finally out, after a couple of days heavy rain. As I passed Lee's office, and the phone was ringing. The sound of the phone making the only noise in the shop. Lee was out for this week, so I was left in charge. I walked into the office and sat in his chair. The phone never rang, so this was exciting. As I reached for the handset Drew walked into the office and sat down. I picked up the phone.

"Hello, maintenance." I greeted.

The voice on the other end was a grumpy man, not impressed that it took so many rings for his call to be answered.

"Sorry, I was out in the yard and didn't hear the phone." I explained. "How can I be of assistance?" I asked.

The man's voice changed to an angry bark as he explained that one of the workers was out on hole number nine.

"And what were they doing out there?" I asked.

I was then told of how the one worker had been driving up and down the cart path and splashing through a puddle that had formed where the path transitions into the grass.

"How many times have they, splashed in the puddle?" I inquired.

"They must have gone back and forth a dozen times, at least," the man complained. "What are you going to do about it?" the angry voice on the other line demanded.

"Well, I will find out who it was and make sure they are fired on the spot." I said a big grin forming on my face.

Drew sat up straight in his chair, easily hearing the conversation, as the person on the other end was loud.

"And then we will beat them with a stick, just so they know how terrible a crime they have committed." I exaggerated.

The voice on the other end gasped at my suggested form of a ridiculous capital punishment.

"Thanks for letting me know," I said, and hung up the phone before they could interject any objections. I had a big grin on my face.

"Well," I said looking at drew. "I guess I'm going to have to fire," I paused for dramatic effect. Drew leaned in closer, anxious to hear who was going to get the axe. "My self." As I bust into laughter.

"Fuck that guy, get fired for driving through a puddle, as if." I stood up from Lee's chair to reveal my pants were soaking wet from the knees down from the back splash of the massive puddle. Drew and I laughed. By now the others had gathered in the doorway, not wanting to miss out on a laugh. I explained the complaint and the required punishment. The team had a good laugh. We all went into the lunchroom to have a quick snack. As we finished up, I made an adjustment to the afternoon assignments.

"Before you all go back to your regular duties, I must insist that you go past hole nine and try out that puddle." The room erupted with enthusiasm at the idea of upsetting a whinny homeowner. We all rushed out to our machines. We formed a caravan of carts and mowers and paraded our way to the ninth hole. Each of us driving through the water, laughing as it sprayed out of the puddle. The vehicles all going their own way after the vengeance was completed. I continued down the ninth fairway, looking back to see a man standing in the window of the house directly in line with the puddle, his arms crossed. I'm sure he was not impressed that his complaint was met with such little regard. I drove on satisfied that vengeance was mine. Driving through deep puddles and making the water splash out is one of the small joys of life, and I have a weakness for puddles.

Chapter 41: Animal Control

I was sitting in lee's office, doing a double check of the time sheets, when the phone rang. It never rings and the sudden break to my concentration had caused my feet to leave the floor. I took a moment to refocus from the startle and answered the phone.

"Hello, maintenance." I greeted.

It was early and the sun was not even up yet. Who could have a complaint this early.

"Hi, I would like to report a coyote." A soft lady's voice explained.

"Ok, and where is the coyote?" I asked puzzled. "And what would you like me to do about it?"

"Well, it's over here on the seventeenth fairway, walking along the fence, and I want you to come get it." "I don't want to leave my dog in the yard with it out there." The lady on the phone spoke with fear in her voice.

"I'm sorry, we are not animal control." I explained. "The coyote is a wild animal and has every right to be out there." "If you see them out there, don't leave your dog in the yard unattended." I hung up the phone and went back to my paperwork.

Once the sun was up, I got into my cart and drove down to the seventeenth fairway looking for the beast. Normally if you

stood still and listened. He reported that a second plane had crashed in New York. Into the same building, the twin towers. This was not an accident. I listened to every word, not moving a muscle. I was filled with a numb sadness over something that had just happened 3800 kilometres away. Standing there on the course I knew that the world had changed. September 11, 2001, would be a day that the world will never forget.

The news of the plane crash took over the radio for the rest of the day, there was no more music, just reports of the death and destruction that had been caused. Speculation was wild. No one knew how or why this had happened. It would take days and weeks to get some solid answers on the cause of this tragedy. Each new report updated the number of casualties. I went back to the shop, my head spinning. It was strange that something so far away had such an effect, but I walked around in a dreamy haze for the rest of the day. Once the workday had finished, I went home, still reeling from the events that occurred on the other side of the country. When I got home and turned on the TV, I got to see the video of the incident. It played on repeat, on every channel. I watched in horror as the planes hit the buildings. Smoke trailing out the windows after impact. After watching the story cycle back to the beginning, I went and had a hot shower. Using the time under the hot water to try and make sense of what I had just watched.

Going through the motions of normality I got dressed. It was Tuesday, normally we would go to the movies. That was the plan at the start of the day, so that's what we did. I picked up Erin and we went to the theatre. The shows were playing at the mall theatre. It had its own doors and could only be entered from outside the mall. We went up to the ticket counter and got tickets for Rock Star. It had opened on Friday, and we would always go see the newest movie on the Tuesday. The theatre was quiet, not empty, but not as busy as the weeks before. We got our snacks and rushed into the theatre to pick our seats. You needed to arrive early to get the best ones. We did not have many other patrons to challenge for seats, half were already taken. We found a good pair in the middle. The seats on either side of us were empty. We snuggled into each other. A few moments later the lights dimmed, and the curtains opened. The sound of the projector filled the theatre before the trailers started. Then the feature started, then ended. Two hours had passed, and I had not absorbed a single frame of the movie. I just sat there, staring off through the screen. My mind was blank, not filled with some deep retrospective thoughts from the day. Just blank.

I wandered through the rest of the week like that, not lost, but with no real direction. After about ten days I started to feel normal again. The world had some time to come to grips with what had happened. More information was coming out all the time. I wasn't filled with fear of the "what ifs" or "what's next." Just an acceptance that the world changed, and that what was, will never be again.

Even now as I write this the events of that day linger in my mind. Knowing some of the stories of the heroics of the plane passengers who tried to stop the catastrophe. To the first responders on the ground who risked their lives to help save survivors. Knowing now that the first responders were exposed to harsh environmental conditions that caused future sickness and death. The toll of that day will be felt for generations. Every now and then it comes up,

Space For Golf

"Where were you on 9-11." I recall the day standing on the green and the sadness I felt.

Chapter 43: 2001 the Final Season

I had spent the winter working at a computer store across town. Once the course reopened, I would work at the course during the day, and after a short trip home and a hot shower, I would work evenings at the computer store. The store started out as a fun place to work but quickly evolved into a goat rodeo. I got the job through one of the people I had met at university, Alan was looking for some new staff and I was looking for a second job. It was a perfect fit. The other staff thought that we were best friends, as I was introduced as someone Alan had went to school with. They had no reason to think that we barely knew each other. I never made the correction as the results played out my favor. I would arrive at the store around five o'clock. I would be hungry from a long day, as I had not had a chance to grab any food as I rushed home from the course to quickly have a shower and change. Then it took a forty-minute drive to the store. On each of my shifts, on my arrival I would walk up to the cashiers and take one of the cute girls out for dinner. We would take about an hour, and when we returned, I would get to doing some work. No one ever questioned me on these dinners, the perceived relationship with the management shielded me from inquires. This went on for months.

Just before Christmas I decided to part ways as the store. It was filled with knuckle heads and had become an embarrassment to work at. The behavior of the computer salesmen had turned childish and unacceptable.

I was one of the cahiers and had a great view of the whole store from the front-end position. I watched as one of the older salesmen, who was working on getting a customer a new pc, was approached by one of the younger salesmen. The younger man stopped in front the other, asked a question, and then punched the older man right in the balls. The old man dropped to his knees and howled. The younger ran off towards the back room. Once the older man had regained his balance the sale was abandoned, and the chase was on. Those two idiots chased each other around the isles, knocking over the game displays and making a scene. Finally, the Manager stepped in and pulled them apart. The younger one got a two-week suspension for his shameful attack. His punishment was expected to be enough for him to never return, but he was not smart enough to take the hint and returned in two weeks.

After that I was finished. It was embarrassing to be part of such a circus. And the drive to the store was turning into more effort than it was worth.

Over the winter Lee's health had taken a turn. All the progress he made on defeating the prostate cancer was overshadowed by a more aggressive cancer that attacked him everywhere else. I walked into his office on my first day back; Lee was behind his desk coughing. I approached to make sure he was alright. Lee lowered his hand revealing a plastic knob sticking out of his neck. My eyes widened at the sight of the extra hole in his neck.

"Are you all right?" I asked.

Lee took a gasp of air, giving a half-hearted smile. "I'll be fine." His voice a raspy whisper.

I sat down across the desk from him. No need to ignore the elephant in the room, so I just asked.

"What's with the thing in your neck?" I leaned in closer to hear him speak.

"The cancer, got into my throat and lungs." He explained. His voice just a whisper. Lee started to rummage the top of his desk looking for something. After a few moments he found what he wanted. Raising his hand up to his neck and pressing a silver device to his throat. "I got this talk box, to help me speak." His voice projected with a creepy robotic tone. "I sound like a robot, and I hate it." He explained. The robotic voice was funny, and I gave him a smile. He lowered the talk box and explained to me in his whispered tone that he still had lots of fight in him and not to worry. I kept a brave face and agreed that his survival was the only option. The tracheostomy was done to help put air into his lungs. There was a tube inserted into his windpipe and this helped him breath.

The weeks went by, and I spent most days with Lee running errands. We would go and pickup parts to repair broken golf carts and whatever else was required. Lee liked to drive, so I would sit in the passenger seat of the old truck. It was hard to watch as a friend diminished right in front of your eyes. As we would drive, Lee would cough and hack, letting go of the steering wheel to retrieve his cloth. I would reach over and grab the wheel to keep the truck moving in straight line. The coughing would launch a thick mucus out of the neck hole. Once all the mucus was blasted through, Lee would catch his breath and regain control of the steering wheel. His lungs were producing a thick bile and the hole in his neck was the only way for it to be dispelled. It was gross, but he was surviving. It was a small price to pay.

The team was supportive and tried to never treat him differently. We would still make jokes and laugh. If Lee was struggling to give us instructions, I would hold my fist up to my neck. Making a fake robot voice telling him to get the voice box so we could understand him. He would smile and pull it out of his pocket to give out the robotic directions. He would always smile, knowing that we teased him out of love.

The summer was hot, and fall was right around the corner. Lee's health took a turn for the worse as the leaves started to change. This was going to be his last season one way or another. Lee spoke of retirement and hopes of spending the next few years fishing. We all knew this was wishful thinking, but we supported the dream. Telling him future stories of the river monsters he would be sure to catch.

Then one morning in late September we were informed that Lee was in the hospital. Drew and I got in the green truck and drove down to see him. The hospital was across town, and we took our time. Fearful of what awaited us on arrival. We went in and got directions to his room. Entering the room with caution, we approached his bed. Lee was sitting up watching TV. He looked not bad for being in the hospital. He told us not to worry and said he would be back at the shop in no time. We didn't stay too long, leaving as soon as the doctor arrived. We left the hospital returning to the course.

The boys were in the shop waiting for an update on Lee's condition. We didn't know much but didn't expect him to return to work anytime soon. Lee was sent home from the hospital a few days later, and as expected never fully returned to work. Lee would show up for quick visits most weeks. His energy drained quickly and would force him to return home to rest. He was stubborn and refused to have the cancer be his defeat.

It was October and the leaves were falling off the trees and the season was starting to be wined down. The golf course was seasonal job, and this season was coming to a close at the end of the month. Monday morning Lanny was waiting for me in the shop as I arrived. Not wanting to repeat the failure of his last mole, he tried a different approach. Lanny flat out said that Blair was going to be in charge for the rest of the season.

Lee would not be returning. I didn't put up any objections and walked away. We knew what to do anyway. So, Blair was, more or less, an empty figure head. There was no need to have a conflict, it was too early in the day. Lanny left with his small victory, and we all went to work.

The first week without went without any problems. The second week we were all asked to head over to the golf dome.

This was an inflatable driving range that was also owned by the golf course, and it needed some work done inside. We were the work force, so we left on an adventure.

The dome is a pressurised balloon. An airlock is used to keep it inflated. You need to open one door, have it close, only then you are able to open the second door. The second door will not open if the first is not sealed properly. The atmosphere forms a vacuum, and the door will not budge while under the pressure. We spent the next few weeks rolling out new artificial turf on the indoor range. Revitalizing it for the winter players to utilize. It was nice to be working inside as the temperature outside was starting to fall, and the morning air was downright cold.

As the end of the month got closer, I started to object to us being at the dome. We needed to have the straw placed over the greens by Halloween. The hay bails had been delivered and were waiting to be broken down over the short grass to protect against the upcoming winter snow. Lee always had us do this before Halloween. He had stories of kids setting the bails on fire on Halloween and we didn't want to take the chance. However my voice went unheard, and we were instructed to continue to be at the dome. I didn't complain, the dome was climate controlled and warm, and the fall air was cold. The season was almost over and I had made plans.

Monday morning the phone at my house started to ring. My mother answered, Blair was on the other end.

"Thomas didn't show up for work today." He said, annoyed.

My mother informed him that I was at work. I had left in the morning with my dad. I had been planning to work for him over the winter. She explained to him that the golf course was seasonal work, and that I had made arrangements to start a new job on November first. Blair was not impressed. None of the boys had showed up. The season was over for us.

"Who is going to put out all the straw over the greens." He asked.

My mother informed him that it was not going to be me and hung up the phone. I had been telling him for weeks that this task needed to be done. I had no guilt, for not being the one to do the work. Blair had my input for weeks and chose not to act on it. It was no longer my problem. I had made the choice that this would be my last season anyway. I wouldn't work for anyone but Lee. Every other previous season ended on the first of November, and this one was no different.

I worked the winter for my father. I was assembling screw conveyors and getting my hands dirty turning wrenches. I was still Seeing Erin, and we would go out on the weekends. She like to go to the bars, so we did. On a couple of occasions, we would go to concerts on a Sunday night. I would get home ridiculously late but still drag myself to work on Monday. Eventually her family moved across town, to the farthest edge of the city. We drifted apart and broke up. I moved on.

I got word on February 23rd 2002, that Lee had passed away. The cancer had engulfed his entire body, working its way into his bones. His cancer battle was bravely fought until the end and he finally found his peace. The funeral was in Stettler, Alberta, the place where Lee was born. Drew and I went with my family for the service. Blair was there to pay his respects. The room was somber as we reflected on the past. Those five years spent at the course with Lee and the boys we the best summers. The work might have been physical and not overly challenging on the mind, but the lessons I learnt, and the friendships I built would shape me forever. I look back fondly on those days as some of the best of my life. I miss Lee all the time and continue to use his teachings while trying to be the best version of myself. His style of leadership has helped me find success within my other opportunities, and I try to pass along his teachings wherever possible.

Conclusion - Epilogue

Over the years we would have family golf tournaments, and on those days, I would return to the course. The one year we were playing a serious family tournament. Dad was up to hit off the ninth tee box. I stood behind him, far enough not to get struck by the back swing and waited for the perfect moment. Dad was on his cancer drugs and was easy to wind up. He swung and struck the ball. It launched high into the air and got lost in the clouds, it was a good shot. As he raised his hand to shield his eyes from the bright sky, I rolled a new ball between his legs. It stopped close to the position of the ball he had just hit. As his eyes slowly adjusted to the sky, he gave up on finding the ball in the distance and bent down to retrieve his wooden tee. As he reached the ground he found the ball. His brain misfired, and he had a moment of full-on confusion. He had just watched the ball soar through the air. Didn't he? We were all laughing at him as he looked over, concerned.

He stammered as he asked, "I hit the ball, didn't I?"

We all roared at the simple trick that was played.

The years I spent working outside at the course were truly the best. I fondly remember them as the good old days. I should spend more time out there making space for golf.

Other Titles Available

SPACE
FOR
GOLF

WRITE YOUR SECOND BOOK IN 236 STEPS
OR LESS

Six Lives Left
Hey! Where Are My Shoes?